NORTH CAROLINA
STATE BOARD OF COMMUNITY
LIBRARIES
SAMPSON TECHNICAL COLLEGE

I'M DOING MY BEST...
BUT IT ISN'T ENOUGH.

CHOICES AND COPING STEPS
FOR PERSONAL DILEMMAS
BY
DR. PAT KEATING

Copyright © 1986 by Pat Keating

All rights reserved. No part of this book may be reproduced in any form or by any means, electronic or mechanical, including photocopying or by any informational storage or retrieval system, without written permission from the copyright owner.

International Standard Book Number
0-931494-82-6

Library of Congress Catalog Card Number
85-72690

First Original Edition
Published in the United States of America

by

Brunswick Publishing Company
Lawrenceville, Virginia

I'M DOING MY BEST...
BUT IT ISN'T ENOUGH.

DEDICATION

To Carrie and Phil for subtleties of choices.
To Mary and John, my exemplars in handling stress.
To Kay for our dilemmas shared and surmounted.
To mentors from a distance, Richard Lazarus and Irving Janis, for their wisdom.
Finally, to the many persons, nameless here, whom I have had the opportunity to help and whose real dilemmas showed the difference between what works and what does not.

It should be noted that the cases presented herein are composites rather than actual descriptions, for purposes both of illustration for the reader and concealment of identities.

CONTENTS

Preface 9

Chapter One
Personal Dilemmas Are
Two-Headed Monsters 21

Chapter Two
Five Steps to Take When You
Don't Know Where to Turn 33

Chapter Three
From Groping to Coping
— by Three SOS Beacons 57

Chapter Four
Getting a Hold On Your Problem 72

Chapter Five
Decisions: on Actions and Attitudes 92

Chapter Six
The Distressful Dilemmas Of Feelings 114

Chapter Seven
Preparing For Your Unique Stress:
Death and the Rest 142

Chapter Eight
Distresses Predictable From Your Own
Attitudes. Overload and Competition 156

Chapter Nine
Dilemmas Needing Your Initiative 180

Chapter Ten
Toughing Out a Distress Which Will
Not Vanish Nor Diminish 196

PREFACE

"I'M DOING MY BEST BUT IT ISN'T ENOUGH"

One of the most common experiences people have today is to face a personal problem which they simply cannot solve. They are people-without-solutions. And you know you are one of the people-without-solutions when you find yourself saying, "I've tried everything but nothing works." Or, "I'm at the end of my rope." Or, "I just don't know where to turn." In some way, you have said, "I'm doing my best but it isn't enough."

You are in a dilemma, a problem which seems incapable of a satisfactory solution. *You are between a rock and a hard place!*

Your own personal dilemma is, of course, special to you. Yet, because many people face situations similar to yours, you can recognize yourself in some of their difficulties. You may be like Turmoil Ted, torn to pieces inside because of all his deadlines at work. Or you may be like Muddling Martha, totally puzzled about what to do about a marriage problem. Perhaps you're like a Hassled Russ, who is passed over for a job or a Conflicted Connie who is torn between wishes of her parents and the demands of her lover. Maybe you are going through the fears of changing from being married to being a divorced person and feel like a Shy Guy. Some people simply and purely feel like Bored Bosco.

Whatever the exact situation, one thing is clear when you are in the middle of a dilemma. You feel as if you are muddling through the middle of a problem which has no solution, no ray of hope, no light at the end of the tunnel.

Certain particular situations bring on the feeling that you have no solutions to your problems:

　　*Personal failures and defeats —
　　*Outworn decisions —
　　*Feelings out of control —
　　*Job hassles —
　　*Family conflicts —
　　*Competition —

*Boredom and loneliness —
*Separations and changes —

You may know what kind of problem I am talking about. They are any of those situations when we feel nonplussed, or stopped short, unable to go any further because no choices seem to be open to us.

This book is a book of solutions. It is an attempt to open up choices where you thought there were none. It is an effort to provide you with steps to take when you feel that very nonplussed state within you. It is meant to help you when you are puzzled and seem to be just muddling through.

In short, this book is a book on helping you make personal decisions. It will offer choices, strategies, aids, check-lists and even "maps" for personal decisions. I will also make some suggestions on attitudes to re-shape and practical steps to take.

Dilemmas in need of our decision are all around us. People have come to describe their state of being without solutions in many ways: their crises, predicaments, quandries and so forth. But no single word is used more often for dilemmas than *stress*. It is our stress which needs our decisions most of all.

Consider the following people, each of whom feels that he or she has a problem for which no solution can be found. They are all at a point of being in a stalemate, an impasse and feel that there is no way out. Yes, they are in stress.

> Gene faces a dilemma of pressures from many sides. He is a single parent of two children from a previous marriage, with a full-time job and going to school part-time. His aging parents have just come to live with him, almost forcing themselves upon him. His mother has just had heart surgery and needs constant care. His father has diabetes. Gene, in addition to work, parenting and school must do all the cooking and housekeeping. He is overwhelmed with the work of caring for three generations of his family. He feels, "I'm doing my best but it's not enough."
>
> Joanne is in a dilemma in a love relationship. She is a forty-year-old woman who has been dating a fifty-

I'm Doing My Best . . . But It Isn't Enough

year-old man for five years. She loves him but he continues to delay. He was married before and now dreads making another mistake; he is indecisive, although he claims that he loves Joanne and then backs away. She has gone to great lengths to assure him that her love is genuine and that prospects for marriage are good. She has even taken a marriage preparation course. He is highly motivated in his work, with strong chances for advancement and at times shows genuine qualities of being a good partner. Still, he is often emotionally abusive by neglect, ridicule and indecision. Joanne says, "I'm at the end of my rope."

Dan's dilemma is on his job. His company is cutting back on sales people. In order to make his quotas, he must work six to seven days a week making contacts. He is often up at night until two A.M. doing paperwork. He recently received word from his supervisor that he is obnoxious to other workers and they refuse to work with him. "Either improve your social skills," he is told, "or we'll be letting you go." Dan doesn't know where to turn.

Shelia has a dilemma at work. She has been passed over twice for promotion. Now, her company has been re-organized and she has been given a position which is, in fact, a demotion. She recently discovered that she has a malignant tumor and her strength is lessened. While some of her colleagues appreciate both her difficulties and efforts, others refuse to believe she cannot do the work anymore. They act hostllely toward her, criticize her and generally make her feel that she is a second-classed workor "who cops out." Shelia does not know what to do. She is totally confused and feels alone.

Donna is in a familiar dilemma. She discovers her husband of 16 years has had an affair with another woman for the past nine months. Her husband admits to caring deeply about the "affair person," but thinks he still loves Donna more. Actually, both

Donna and her husband have their own dilemmas. The choices of divorce, separation, or staying together do not help them decide. They are indecisive, continually in emotional turmoil and don't know where to turn.

HOW STRESS BECOMES *DISTRESS*

I have introduced that loaded word, "stress." Perhaps you are tired of hearing about it, or at least of solutions to it. Stress has become an overused word, meaning every imaginable hassle and worry. Stress has come to be a "buzz word," a faddish way of describing problems. Let me reassure you, this is *not* just another book about stress.

Stress, as you have probably heard, is usually meant to refer to *pressure* and *tension*. Stress has come to be associated with the pressure of deadlines at work, overload, balancing too many things, meeting too many demands. Stress is any of these things, but *it is more.*

Stress may also be used to refer to a young mother supporting her children alone as a domestic. It is applied to the experience of living in a world of "future shock" and computers, of fast change and anonymity. Stress can be expressed in a person who is walking down a dimly lit street while being followed by "toughs." Stress has been applied to anyone's struggle to live from paycheck to payment, to put up with an irritating job, or to live in an embittered home environment. Stress has become *stretched* to mean everything — and therefore nothing, somewhat like anxiety and depression. It can be argued that the word has simply become the name that people today give to their problems — simply that and no more.

But stress can be much more than pressure and tension, or a new trendy way to describe problems. There are special problems today in a sense stressful that I will later describe. As a recent ad said, "Life got stronger and we got tougher." But when stress becomes *more* than pressure and tension, it becomes *distress.*

A book with the significant title, *Stress Without Distress* that appeared a few years ago, was written by a man in some ways responsible for much modern talk about "stress." His

I'm Doing My Best . . . But It Isn't Enough 13

name is Hans Selye and he used the word stress as it applied to human reactions. From Dr. Selye came the valuable idea of stress as being a "nonspecific response of the body to any demand made upon it." Since his work, people have talked about stress mainly as pressure and tension.

This book is very different. It is about stress *with* distress; indeed about how stress becomes distress. To see how stress becomes distress one must look again at a few of the personal dilemmas that were described a bit earlier. Each of these persons was harassed but there was more than the *feeling* of harrassment. Each had a dilemma which included stress, but also a whole lot more.

Gene, for example, needed more than exercises on how to relax. He was confused and needed help in making some decisions to resolve being overwhelmed — he was *distressed*, not merely stressed. Joanne needed more than to change her diet and "get away for a bit"; she needed to make a hard decision about her boyfriend of five years. Dan is typical of many business persons who need more than "stress training" in relaxation, time-management and social skills. He was distressed about some choices he had to make and what steps to take. The situation of Shelia was similar. Donna and her husband had the distress of years of marriage, which now took a distinct turn. Matters could never be the same. Choices had to be made and steps had to be taken. Thus, your problems too are probably more than stress on occasion. They are dilemmas which require you to do something — often you do not know quite what. With more than pressure and tensions you have *distress.*

EXPERIENCING PERSONAL DILEMMAS: DISTRESS

The distress of a personal dilemma is a very special experience. You yourself have doubtlessly shared in it, not exactly as Gene or Joanne but you have felt unable to solve a personal problem. You have felt the pressure and tension of stress, but your difficulty seemed so much more. Suppose we draw out the personal experience of dilemma. What is the experience of being without a solution? What happens to one when, beyond being tense, one has the distress of a dilemma? There seem to be four features to one's state of mind? *confused, hopeless, isolated,* and *physically upset.*

If we were to summarize what one feels when without a solution to a personal problem, that one word might be *confusion*. One shows this confusion in the way he or she feels and thinks and acts. Especially this confusion is noticed in the way one behaves. It is almost frightening. He may break into a rage, screaming and yelling followed by a shouting match. Or he or she may collapse into tears, sobbing heavily, and if asked what the trouble is, would answer, "Oh, just everything! I don't even know why. I'm just so confused." Or one may become apathetic, without any energy at all, knowing there is something he or she *should* be doing but does not know what. Or perhaps he is the kind of person, who, when confused, acts at random, attacking problems in a shot-gun fashion, with no rhyme or reason. Nothing done is very effective. So a person without a solution to a personal problem first shows it in confusion.

A second thing about a person without a solution is that he or she sees things as hopeless. He or she sees no light at the end of the tunnel (except a train coming the other way, as the quip has it). There seems to be no chance of things getting any better. He or she feels pessimistic, gloomy, and doomed. All he can see is that his project will not be acceptable, or his or her job application will not be approved, or money will not hold out so bills can be met, or health will not get better, and on and on and on.

If there is one thing most in need of changing for a person up against a tough problem, it is the pessimism he feels. Yet nothing is hard to change. Things may look gloomy, but one forgets that it will all change *sometime*. One even forgets that one once felt better.

Then there is the third feeling for one without a solution: loneliness. Not only does one feel there is nowhere to turn; but also there is no *one* to turn to. One begins to feel that his or her hurt is unique, so special that no one has ever gone through it before. Never mind the statistics of how many others have gone through a divorce, gone through a job failure, had difficulty at home, and so on. What seems to soak in is that "My problem is like no other," which in one sense is true, but this feeling takes on the proportions of being a total fallacy.

I'm Doing My Best... But It Isn't Enough

Then one feels alienated from all others — especially those who could help.

Another aspect of this feeling alone is that it can make a person think that no one else *cares*. "They all have their own problems. They don't want to be bothered with mine." Not only does one feel isolated but may also hold back from seeking others because he thinks they are not interested, or that he is not worth their attention. He builds no walls between himself and other people instead of building bridges.

The fourth mark of a person without a solution is that he or she feels so upset physically, that he or she will do anything to feel better: pop a valium, get a hold of a new upper or downer. He or she will do anything to get rid of the headache, the floating uneasiness, and maybe the difficulty in breathing.

Being physically upset — to most of us this is fact *one* of having a problem without a solution. This is *stress*, about which so much is said today. "Stress" has come to be the one word which people use to summarize *pressure and tension*. One knows this tension in himself or herself as he or she personally experiences it, which may be somehow different from the way other people experience the physical state of stress. A person picks out those sensations most familiar to him or her, from the following list:

  *pains in the chest
  *stiffness or tightness in the back of the neck
  *nervous movements in hands, arms, legs
  *difficulty in breathing
  *feeling that stomach is tied up in knots
  *pain in the stomach or even ulcers
  *sleeplessness
  *general weakness in the body
  *coldness in hands or in the feet
  *light-headness or faintness

And he or she has thoughts which indicate tension:

  *thinking that he or she is falling apart
  *mixing up thoughts resulting in confusion
  *thinking that something should be done but not being sure what to do

*thinking he or she cannot cope
*getting upset by little things which really should not matter

And so one knows his or her own form of "stress."

A VERY MODERN PROBLEM: DISTRESS

In modern dilemmas, therefore, people experience some very modern states of mind and body. Confusion, hopelessness, feeling isolation and tension: these are the symptoms of modern life, when stress has flowered into distress because of not having a solution to a problem. Most people face dilemmas today which seem to have no quick fix, no ready answer, no facile solution.

It is worth pausing a moment to see just how special experiences of distress are. Just what exactly makes peoples' problems so special today? Surely we are not special for being worried, tense, having pressures, feeling upset, depressed and overburdened! People have always had these troubled reactions, so no one is unique in experiencing them.

Consider the pioneers and as far back as you might care to go; people have always been plaqued with worries and feelings of tension. For these reactions, the same people have developed healing remedies. They developed potions and herbs, bleedings and tonics, for everything from stomach cramps, backaches, headaches, fears and heart ailments. No, people today are not the first to experience pressure and tension.

The biggest difference perhaps between people today and earlier peoples is this: they at least *knew* what they needed and wanted, and what a solution to their problems would look like. Their problems were not easy but they were clearer. People today, on the other hand, are so enmeshed in change, future shock, value upheavels, weakened social institutions, and international business and economic pressures that are not as sure of what their real wants are nor of even what a solution to their needs might look like.

Stress has become distress. Problems have gone beyond pressure and tension. Today's difficulties are unique and can be seen as such by examining a few basic rules of

I'm Doing My Best... But It Isn't Enough

human life. The first rule is *much of what a person finds distressing depends upon what he considers threatening.* What a person considers threatening, in turn, depends upon what a person values. Stress and distress are somewhat in the eye of the beholder. These are particularly distressing days because values are for many people unclear.

Generally in times of pure stress, the more threatening something is, the more a person's belief system comes into play to guide him or her. But today many people have not come up with a belief system. Thus they feel unable to make needed decisions. They further feel very vulnerable. People today often do not know what a solution would look like because they do not know what they want or need.

Secondly, that people today live in uniquely distressing times can be seen in another rule of human life: *The more ambiguous matters are the greater will be the stress and distress.* Stress has become distress of dilemmas because at no time have lives been so complicated and ambiguous. Ambiguity has become so intensified that stress has become distress. Old ways no longer work. Hard work, for example, used to be enough for the small business person, but not so today, since his efforts are offset by forces he can neither see nor control — such interest rates, the stock market, embargoes, mergers, and on and on.

But stress has become distress for a third reason. *At the heart of distress and dilemmas there is the feeling of being threatened.* Stress steps beyond pressure and tension with one word: $THREAT$. A threat endangers what one wants or needs or desires. It is a threat which puts us at risk, and fills us with confusion, hoplessness, isolation and physical turmoil.

"Threat" seems to lump together most of the worries, dreads, anticipations, impending hurts and indeed all the moaning of the future. "Threat" is the one word which summarizes and discloses what bothers people today in their own person, their families, their jobs, and even throughout the government and economic system. Time and time again young people go into drugs because "What difference will it make to study and work hard? The bomb will destroy us anyway." They live under the threat of "the bomb," and they are symbols of us all. Days are surrounded more by threats and future anticipations than any time before.

Today is a unique day of distressful dilemmas. Most of the "stresses" deal with threats about the future, its expected losses and opportunities. For example, most of the concerns are such things as worrying whether the next payment can be made on homes, whether or not members will be laid off, whether or not some harmony will be restored in families, how the children will turn out, how people can cope with divorce, or retirement, or provide for the education of children, and on and on. Man lives, with the distress of the *future* more than with the stress of the present; more with the threats of dilemmas than with pressure and tension.

True, there are the brutal conditions of being unemployed *now*, the tar and cement and crime of inner cities now, of the child in trouble now — not what *may* be. Still is it not the threats (of even these) which trouble us most? Do we not live more with the hassles of anticipation than with actual confrontation?

A stress is the agony of being without a home now; it is having one's life ravaged by a tornado or being with no food now. This is a terrible thing and a matter of pressure and tension. But for most people, the agonies look into the future and what *might* happen if or unless, changes are made.

In summary, people live today in a unique time where they face dilemmas of not knowing what to do, in a time when, more than having the stress of pressure and tension there is the distress of making some decisions. This unique experience is that of a well-warranted state of confusion, hopelessness, isolation and physical upset. Lives are filled with ambiguous complexities and threats which come faster than can often be anticipated. And, if people happen to be unsure of their wants or values, they have all the greater dosage of distress and dilemmas.

There are different ways to emerge from dilemmas. People can come out of present dilemmas the same as they went into them, but they can also come out of them worse than before. On the other hand, they might also come out of them better than before — if they take the right coping steps and make the right choices.

The latest dilemma that must be faced will not be the last. There will be again similar ones to meet. This book is about

I'm Doing My Best... But It Isn't Enough

making choices, arriving at decisions in distressful dilemmas and then on how to take the right steps to emerge stronger and better — more skilled and more apt, more confident and more ready to handle the threats which make life today so different and more demanding than at any other time. Future decisions may depend on what is learned from this book.

Chapter One

Personal Dilemmas Are Two-Headed Monsters

If you are in a dilemma right now and feel you have tried everything but nothing works, you may want to skip this chapter and go right to Chapter Two: "Five Steps When You Don't Know Where To Turn." Practical advice is given there for you to make sure you are doing some of the right things. That chapter is for a person who needs to act *now*. If, on the other hand, you have a little bit of time, you will be better prepared for dealing with your dilemma by reading this chapter prior to going to the next one.

A MOMENT OF QUIET

I hope that at this point you are able to be somewhat relaxed. I hope that perhaps you are rested and not quite so upset with a dilemma that you cannot take your mind off it for a moment. What I will be saying here is very important, but strangely, is best grasped when you do not have an immediate, pressing problem; instead you are preparing for a time when you do have a dilemma.

The best time to learn how to deal with stress and distress is in time of quiet — before feelings are churned and outlooks are blurred. Modern science tells us this very important rule of thumb when handling problems: *Our most effective skills are those acquired under little or no pressure.* It is when we are relaxed that our flexibility is highest, our openess to improvement is greatest and we are the most agile for finding new solutions when before we thought there were none. Clearest outlooks and sharpest skills surface in a concentration which is undistracted and undisturbed. Stress and distress need a moment of calm.

THE KEY TO STRESS AND DISTRESS

A moment of calm before a stress will teach you one thing more, and when learned, makes sense of all anyone can say about stress. I myself learned it in a moment of calm. I had been in the area of understanding and helping people in stress for about twelve years at the time. I had just given a workshop on stress to labor union leaders. We had dealt with their worries of threats such as facing membership meetings and conflicts created at home. We developed abilities to deal with people and to relax, the advantage of group meetings along with bull and gripe sessions; we addressed their long hours, their fatigue and burnout. Then a most important key to stress and distress came to my mind.

I happened to have an hour of leisure time after the workshop and went over the experience in mind. Only then did I learn something which I now think is crucial for all of us coping with stress. Stress is a *two-headed monster*, and much of the time people spend talking about only one head. As a result, much of what they suggest, sensible though it sounds, works only halfway because only one head is faced. I learned about the "two heads" of stress while reflecting on one union leader whom I will call Oliver.

> Oliver was developing an ulcer and drinking excessively as he examined his stress. On the one hand, he felt fearful and anxious about the insecurity of his job. He felt depressed at meeting the expectations of both his family and constituents, and also felt guilt about neglecting these responsibilities. He felt inadequate to provide the leadership demanded of him and to handle the inerpersonal conflicts of his subordinates. On the other hand, Oliver had decisions to make on union policies and regulations, conflicts with workers, dealing with problem people, better use of his own time. But two major decisions were how to reduce harm to his family life and how or when to retire.

In summary, Oliver's stress had two faces: on the one hand, the reactions he was feeling in fears, insecurity, depression, guilt and ulcers and on the other hand, his stress

I'm Doing My Best . . . But It Isn't Enough 23

was almost exactly the same thing as the problems he had to solve, the decisions he had to make. In the first place, his stress left him in an experience of pain, confusion and off-balance. In the second place, his stress was a problem to be solved. Some of his decisions were continual and repetitive (handling meetings or interpersonal conflicts); other decisions were more infrequent but momentous (e.g. when to retire, how to spend more time with his family). *But these are the two faces of stress;* the *painful reactions* we suffer and the *problem* we have to resolve.

Like Oliver, your stress is two-headed. It shows two faces to you. Your problem-without-a-solution shows itself first in ailments and feelings of upset. This is its first face. But the second face is that of some problem to be solved, a solution to be found, a decision to make. Recognizing these two faces of stress is what makes this book special, unlike other books on stress today which mainly address the physical tension and pressure of stress — its first face.

The fact of stress being two-headed is not original with me, though this fact did register in a personal way. This is what eminent stress researchers have found, and I have intensively studied the area for over fourteen years. Great credit for a thorough understanding of real stress (*distress*) goes to Richard Lazarus, one of the giants in the field.

DISTRESS HAS TWO HEADS

Face One: The Wrinkles of Stress. Stress lets itself be known in ailments and sensations from the beginning. Stress shows itself as vividly as the wrinkles in our brow and eyes. Indeed, all of the sensations mentioned earlier might be called "the wrinkles of stress." The first face is therefore our wrinkled face: from the "wrinkles" in blood pressure, headaches, perspiration, stomach aches to ulcers and hypertension. The physical discomforts are the wrinkled face of stress. They cause anguish and perhaps alarm. The wrinkles are not the core of stress, but they surely get our attention! They press for relief. The wrinkles cause us discomfort, but then they also do us the favors of alerting us to a danger and of *motivating* us to do something.

The first face of stress includes those aspects of stress most attended to by popular books and articles. Literary works have for a long time presented the portraits of the "first face" of stress. Novelists have written graphically of the facial pallor of fear, the red flush of shame or anger, and on and on. And Face One is that of which we most want to rid ourselves.

Small wonder that Face One of stress is where most help and suggestions are directed. Face One today is where the relaxation exercises are directed; the awareness experiences, nutrition plans, and time-control tactics are also aimed at Face One of stress. We are fortunate today to have such help for the wrinkles of distress. Since we do live in an age when stress is special (I will go into this later), we also are recipients of much self-help guidance for dealing with the presure and tension of stress, or Face One. I call this help "Short Order Solutions," or the S.O.S. for stress.

SOS aid to stress is very important. The solutions of relaxation, nutrition and the like are of enormous help. I want to be very clear about that with you, the reader. At the end of this chapter is a list of very helpful readings you might wish to use. Further, I will be including many, many SOS aids in helping you cope with stress.

This full acknowledgement being given to the SOS steps for the first face of stress, you need to know your stress requires more. There remains, if you will, the other face of stress: the problem requiring a solution. You will need, as I indicated in the subtitle of this book, choices and steps to *solve* the problem or to make some decisions. The SOS aids are terribly valuable. Still, they are *short* term solutions. You may have noticed that they do not always work for you, at least indefinitely. This is understandable. You will, after all, need to replace the band-aid with a "cure." Sooner or later, you will need to replace the Short Order Solutions with Long Term Solutions.

Long Term Solutions are for the Second Face of Stress.

Face Two of Stress: It Becomes Distress. The entire condition of being in distress can be summarized neatly by a picture of a man in a boat and about to be thrown overboard by a churning, storm tossed lake. His first question is: Can I swim?

I'm Doing My Best . . . But It Isn't Enough

In any severe problem the major question is, *"What can I do?"* If there is the answer, "I don't know" or "Nothing!" then there is the distress of dilemma. A person is then "doing his or her best but it isn't enough." Being in distress of a dilemma is more than being upset; it is having a problem and checking to see what one can do about it.

Back to Oliver. He was more than physically upset, fatigued and worried. He had more than the feelings of insecurity and ulcers. He had to make some decisions. Could he? What could he do, how could he decide? He was searching not only for a way to soften his discomfort, as in a relaxation exercise he was seeking something to *do* to change his situation. He needed to confront the second face of stress, a problem to be solved or a decision to be made. Until he solved the problem, his stress would remain. The "problem" aspect of stress creates a state of *distress*.

So, too, with your stress. It will remain as long as you do not look at the second face, the problem which you need to solve or decide upon. The second face of our stress turns it into distress. By all means use relaxation exercises, improve your diet and get some control of your schedule. But there is more to seek: you will need a solution of something to do.

For Face One, the steps are Short Order Solutions — S.O.S. steps. For Face Two there are those steps which resolve the distress of dilemmas. These include decisions both for attitudes to re-shape and actions to take.

WHAT TOOLS YOUR DILEMMA WILL REQUIRE

Now that you have seen the real key to dealing with your stresses and have recognized that you will need to confront the second face of this stress, you are in a position to prepare yourself to handle your dilemma. What will be required of you to deal with this dilemma?

From our best information you will need three things for coping with your distressful dilemma. There are, if you please, three kinds of equipment. Stress expert David Mechanic has summarized nicely what any person needs in his or her distressful dilemma when he said these three tools seem to be most central.

*The person will need *skills* and capabilities to deal with the demands made upon him/her.

*The person will need some condition of being with *supports,* and able to maintain a steady course.

*The person will require some *motivation,* that is, some aim and goal as well as some interest to do something.

It is the development of these three — skills, supports and motivation — which enables a person to deal best with the dilemma which may face him or her. Let's take a brief look at each of them.

Skills. Far and away the most important tool is the skill to make decisions. As with the man in the boat, the major question for you in your dilemma is, "What can I do?" If a person knows what to do, there is no real problem. If the person knows what to do even though there will be hassles and pressure and tension, the situation will be one of stress raising its First Head.

But if you do not know what to do, if you feel you do not have the skills to deal with the dilemma, you are in the distress of seeing no way out. And then you need decision making skills. So much of the next three chapters is devoted to exactly this, the decision making skills you will require in your dilemma.

Supports. "There are three things in life," it has been said, "that you must do alone: die, testify and putt." Good coping with dilemmas is *not* one of them. Good coping with distress as well as stress requires that we have the support of other people. We need the help, the reassurance and, sometimes, even the guidance of other people. In chapters Three and Four we will become very practical throughout this book on how to depend upon other people.

It should be indicated here that the support of other people is not limited to have someone to whom we can talk about our troubles. In addition to this valuable support, other people can offer us other kinds of support. Their impact can be very great in the accumulated wisdom other people can offer us. We are not the first to cope with stress and distress. However unique and singular we may feel, others have coped with similar dilemmas and how they have dealt with their

I'm Doing My Best . . . But It Isn't Enough

problems can be both an inspiration and instructive to us, even a "map" to follow.

There are other kinds of supports which you will need in your dilemmas, such as resources you can draw upon. These will include Short Order Solutions and other resources which we will discuss in later chapters, particularly chapters Three and Ten and in other chapters as well.

Motives and Aims. In the hurting feeling of your distress you probably have now a decided motivation to deal with your dilemma. That is, curiously, most necessary and even helpful. But it is also important for you to decide upon some goal: on how you want to come out of your distress. Let me show you what I mean by some examples.

DIFFERENT OUTCOMES OF DILEMMAS

Bob, once divorced, has a whirlwind romance with a woman whom he married after three weeks of courtship. After the first weeks of his marriage, he filled his mind with worries about having made a mistake again. Bob talked about his fears to a cousin who had just had a introductory psychology course; his cousin urged Bob to divorce the woman, citing jargon about unresolved complexes and self-defeating dependency on her. Bob filed for divorce. Two months later, however, he changed his mind and wanted to re-marry the woman. They did re-marry but this pact lasted about two years, and they separated again. He still felt attracted to her, saw her regularly during the separation but felt miserable with himself for still seeing her. Bob never learned from his stress, he did not improve but rather got deeper into his negative state.

Donna had been separated from her husband and felt satisfied that it was the proper choice. However, she was having a hard time forgetting her husband because of vindictive and hateful thoughts. These thoughts interferred with her career. She could not concentrate on her work and her business was deteriorating. She had a crisis for which she saw a professional who helped her get rid of unwanted thoughts. When this problem was solved, Donna was able to return to her previous balance of mind. She emerged able to handle her personal matters as well as she could before.

Helen was coping with a recent divorce. She was feeling very empty and hopeless. She joined a group of divorced persons going through the same crisis and learned how to "let go" of any thoughts of reconciliation. She also re-worked her feelings about herself as totally dependent upon her former husband. She emerged able to see herself in a new way — as a person, a woman, professionally and socially. She had new feelings and better skills, with more confidence. She emerged better than she was before.

Bob, Donna and Helen have stresses which help us understand two important things about coping with either stresses or distresses. First, there are different ways to emerge as a person after one's problem:

- *you can come out of your dilemma worse than you went into it (Bob);
- *or, you can come out of it at the same level of functioning that you went into your dilemma (Donna);
- *or, you can come out of your difficulty at a higher level, more skilled and feeling better about yourself (Helen.)

Secondly, the above persons show us that though they all faced the similar stress of divorce, they used different skills and strategies. They used different skills because they each had different *aims,* differing motives toward coping with their problem. The outcomes were the result of their separate aims, though they may not have pictured these aims clearly or consciously to themselves.

The basic question one has to ask oneself is:

- *Do I want to return things to the way they were or do I want to come out of this better than I was before?

That is, "Do I want to restore or to improve my situation?" Being equipped to deal with dilemmas requires more than skill; it takes a desire and the hope of bringing some aim about. This sounds evident but some persons are more motivated to escape problems than to come through them as well as they were before the problem arose. Just as there are different levels of skills, there are different levels of motivations to deal with a dilemma: to come out of it as well or better than before, or to come out of the stress worse. Let me add a word about "aim of coming out worse." Surely, few people consciously aim at this yet many people are defeated and "broken" after a marriage failure, a job loss. They then *avoid* problems: avoidance is their real aim and motive. This avoidance aim takes many forms: by running away from problems literally but also by escaping through alcohol and other drugs, by blaming others and by apathy. Their aim, however, unconscious, leaves them worse after their problem. They are weakened after this problem.

This brings us to a major need for all of us in our problems, whether they be crises, stresses or distresses. Everyone feels at least a bit weakened after these problems. Here is the point where you should know one more skill in coping with your dilemmas and your stresses; this is the *skill of strength-finding*.

STRENGTH-FINDING

If you know that you feel somewhat weakened by stresses and distresses, you should also know *there is a strength you can gain from every stress and distress*. Out of any awareness of weakness arises the need to change and to become someone better. Becoming someone better means, among other things, to become someone stronger. Stresses strangely are a path to personal growth. Distresses and stresses are something like turning points which one experiences as times both of conflict and resolutions, of groping choices and hard decisions, as weakness and as strength. There may be no other way by which people grow most decisively.

I fancy myself a strength-finder. Before we plunge into your stress or crisis, I would submit that it is a strength for you to experience stress at all, even if you should feel that you are not handling it very well.

By saying there is "a strength in your stress," I mean there is a plus or a positive note about anyone experiencing such distress. True, while in a stress this statement sounds elusive if not the gibberish of malarkey. Still, I would suggest the reader take this brief reminder seriously. So where is the plus? The first strength of a stress, any stress at all, is that it discloses our needs. We have stress because we have needs and values and motives — all alerted to us in the stress. We have motives and these are threatened in stress; we have wants and there is a challenge to their being satisfied. We have values which will only be realized through effort. Some persons only realize what they want or can become when faced with divorce, for example.

Secondly, a plus in stress is to tell us about our choices. In each stress there is some *conflict* and conflicts are the start of decision making. Without conflicts we will often not make those choices which are for our best interest. Without conflicts we will not discover new solutions though the old ones are not working anymore. In fact, without conflicts people appear not to find satisfactions in family life which persons reach for — the greatest satisfactions of intimacy.

A third plus of stress is starting to get a bit of press these days. You have perhaps heard that there is a "good kind" of stress, called *eustress* by the very man who brought "stress" into our vocabulary, Hans Seyle. By eustress, he means those challenges we all know we deliberately put into our lives, from checkers to sky diving to career changes to skiing and tough tasks freely chosen. These "stresses" stimulate us, exhilarate us and keep us feeling alive, alert, moving and active.

The "bad kind" of stress is then sometimes called *distress*. But this stress also has a plus. Problems such as those you have come to humans alone and mark the level of your awakeness and awareness. So much of any person's level of consciousness stems from his or her particular problems and conflicts. This is a "plus."? you ask. You might wish you were not so fortunate! But look again. The dreary days of persons who are bored, wasted, withering and neglected are enough to remind us all that it is indeed our problems which keep us at our peak of awareness. It is our stresses which keep us alert, vigilant and in some ways growing.

In sum, it's like the man said: The only difference between a rut and a grave are the dimensions (Goethe, I think). Without problems we would not have those activating moments which take us beyond the ruts. Without conflicts we would be very conventional — flat, stale, and boring as well as bored. Without conflicts we would never change our attitudes or opinions, never become alerted to some of the best features of those less than glorious persons in our lives. And, what is more, without conflicts we would certainly never gain an identity of our choosing.

In brief, the conflict seems to be the single ingredient for achieving personal triumphs of successful marriage, career choices, attitude changes, better solutions to tasks we want done, identity within ourselves and a fondness for those persons who, on the surface, are less than attractive.

Contentment is for cows.

THIS IS A SPECIAL BOOK

To deal with your conflicts and discover your strengths this book has been designed and written. I will present you with solutions, some short-term and others long-term, to your stresses and crisis. You will learn what other people find that works for them and how you can prepare for your own unique stresses. If you are right now in a crisis, Chapter Two through Four were written for you and you might want to go to them immediately. Chapters Five through Ten will help you plan for some long term solutions to your stress.

Helpful Books on Stress

Brief, A. P., Schuler, R. S. & Van Sell, M. *Managing Job Stress.* Boston: Little, Brown and Co., 1981.

Girdanao, D. and Everly G. *Controlling Stress & Tension.* Englewood Cliffs: Prentice-Hall, 1979.

Ivancevich, J. M. and Matteson, M. T. *Stress and Work, A Managerial Perspective.* Dallas: Scott, Foresman and Co., 1980.

Krantzler, M. *Creative Divorce.* New York: Signet, 1975.

Mason, L. J. *Guide to Stress Reduction.* Culver City: Peace Press, 1980.

McQuade, W. and Aikman A. *Stress.* New York: Bantam, 1974.

Schwartz, J. *Letting Go of Stress.* New York: Pinnacle, 1982.

Steinmetz, J., Blankenship, J., Brown, L. Hall, D. and Miller, G. *Managing Stress Before It Manages You.* Palo Alto: Bull, 1980.

Veninga, R. L. and Spradley, J. P. *The Work Stress Connection.* New York: Ballantine, 1981.

Chapter Two

Five Steps to Take When You Don't Know Where to Turn

If you are presently in a dilemma and would like to check out what you should be doing immediately, then this chapter is for you.

GETTING THE PICTURE

"It is difficult to see the picture when you are inside the frame." This could be your motto if you are currently in a distress. When a person is in the middle of a difficult dilemma, it is indeed like being inside the frame and unable to see the total picture. A person needs somehow to step back and get some distance on the problem.

You can get distance on your own problem in two ways: first by viewing other persons in a personal difficulty, noticing how they are affected; second, by going over some concrete steps which have proven helpful to others in their dilemmas. Here are some persons in *crises,* which are really "compressed dilemmas."

> *Russ is in a crisis at work. He has worked in an agency for six years and now the re-organization of staff duties leaves him demoted, with fewer responsibilities and no pay raise. His pain is that he is being humiliated and bypassed. His grief is intensified by his director's explanation that he has been criticized frequently over the years by subordinates and this may be the reason for high turnover of personnel.

*Mary is an eighteen year old with a crisis which she shares with a friend. She does not want to go to school, yet her father insists on it. She feels like a puppet pulled by the strings of her parents. She wants to be independent, get a job and buy things she wants now. She tells her plight to her friend but afterwards feels worse because of her friend's behavior, and Mary leaves in tears.

*Theresa is in a crisis of her aunt who is dying. The stress of her aunt's deterioration is a heavy burden on the family and Theresa particularly feels intensified pressure because she does not know what to say when she visits her aunt; she feels she should know what to say to answer when her aunt asks, "Why me?" Her aunt is only forty-five years old and is filled with hostility about dying.

Each of these persons was in a *crisis*. The "picture" of being in a crisis is that a person does not know where to turn. A crisis means having a difficult choice to make — that's the very meaning of the word.

A crisis tells us a lot about people in stress and distress. In actual fact, a crisis is a "compacted stress." It is a sheer and abbreviated experience of the turmoil, tension and helpless state of affairs we call stress or distress. A crisis is a time when all the ingredients of stress mix together, usually rather suddenly and for a short time. For that reason, a picture of crisis is somewhat harder to come by, for it is such an intense experience.

YOU KNOW YOU ARE IN A CRISIS WHEN . . .

A person in a crisis shows it. He or she is different and shows it:

*in behavior
*in feelings
*in thinking

Some people in a crisis show it as Mary did, in her behavior. After leaving her friend she sat down to try to study, stopped shortly and began making a casserole only to leave the mixings spread out on the table and plopped down before

I'm Doing My Best... But It Isn't Enough

the TV for a while. Soon she "flitted" off to other activities. She became totally random in her behavior. But eventually she became very inactive, and felt depressed without hope. Like anyone in either crisis or distress, Mary showed a change in behavior. She is not ordinarily so "fidgety." People do things out of the ordinary; sometimes they "act out" by doing something they do not ordinarily do, like drink more alcohol, or break into a rage. But they may also become paralyzed. They may crumble into tears, collapse and just do nothing, not even carry out their daily routine. Mary showed her crisis in her behavior by being totally disorganized.

Sometimes a crisis shows up more in one's feelings, as it did with Theresa. She felt everything was so hopeless, that there was nothing she could do about her aunt's situation. She did not think she could avoid her aunt entirely, and indeed wanted to be some comfort to her. Still, what could she say or do for her aunt asking, "Why me?". So feelings come on in an especially powerful way. They may be feelings of depression and feeling "down." Or the feelings may be giving a person the experience of a powder keg about to explode. Very often there will be a state of anxiety and panic — which is blended with the first feature, behavior which is restless.

Thirdly, a crisis will show up in a person's thinking. There is a breakdown in judgement. A person like Russ starts to muddle through his work. He is confused and unable to stick to anything and get a job done or attend with his mind to his work. Reports do not get finished, the phone is not answered, people do not get contacted — as was formerly his manner of carrying out his work. In a word, he gets less effective. A crisis mental state may show itself either by a person being confused and taking on too much, or by becoming constricted in his or her thoughts. That is, he or she may either get widely confused or have tunnel vision. Either way, his or her judgment and *ability to make decisions is impaired*

Perhaps you notice that you are presently affected in your feelings, thoughts or behavior just as the persons above. Now is the time for you to take some steps. What follows are some specific, concrete actions you can take immediately to improve your situation. Often it will be most helpful to take one step at a time in the order suggested here. Most people find there is a natural sequence to carry out in delaing with a crisis. The steps are these:

1) GET IT OUT. Talk about your dilemma to a carefully chosen friend.
2) GET A HANDLE. Try to grasp clearly what the main problem is.
3) GET RID OF RIGIDNESS. Get some perspective; try to see new solutions.
4) REGAIN YOUR STRENGTHS. Gather your resources, personal and in others.
5) GET A PLAN. Make a decision. Do something to take action.

Even these steps are not exactly the same for dealing with every dilemma. For example, a person may feel that before s/he can "get a handle", s/he must first rid him or herself of rigidness by getting relaxed; s/he feels too uptight to see what the main issues are in his or her dilemma.

Nevertheless, this is a helpful way to begin helping yourself. In fact, when we later go on to a variety of particular types of dilemmas, these same steps will help you see that these are practical ways to proceed. Whether there is the distress of a personal emotional turmoil, or work overload, or competitive work situation, these are helpful steps to take.

STEP ONE: GET IT OUT

At the outset of your dilemma you will need to find someone to whom you can talk about your problem. Nothing is perhaps so important as this, to "tell your story" to someone you trust. Having someone to confide in will do a number of things for you. First it will prevent you from that terrible feeling of being all alone. You need good human contact in your dilemma. The isolation you feel needs to be modified by talking with someone. Feeling alone is an easy first thought of any crisis or distress.

A second thing talking things out will do for you is to unbottle your feelings which are welling up inside. You particularly will need to get out feelings of helplessness, vulnerability, hopelessness, and confusion which are part of the great anguish you may be experiencing.

I'm Doing My Best... But It Isn't Enough **37**

The third thing talking to a friend will do is to help you better understand your problem. Just by getting things out into words, problems seem more manageable, conflicts less intolerable, confusion seems less cloudy. A person's stresses and dilemmas are enormously difficult to understand. When all the pressures are compacted into a circle, most people will not be able to understand them without other people.

The fourth thing which talking to a trusted person does is help you understand some strengths you have which you may be forgetting. The more they know you the more they will be able to recall previous situations when you faced a difficulty and solved it. The friend will also be likely to know what resources you can draw on, whom else you can turn to for added support, guidance and even coping ability.

However, this fourth benefit of talking to someone raises an important point about this entire first step of opening up to someone. You have to be selective (*very* selective) about whom you choose. The kind of person you need to talk to needs to be, above all else, a *good listener*. That is, what you need right now is someone who will be receptive, sympathetic, understanding — but not someone who is quick to give advice. Guidance is not what you most need in the beginning but just someone who gives you his or her full attention to receive what you have to say.

So avoid people who are frustrated counselors or who are ready with evaluations, scrutiny, criticisms. Avoid also peole who in their personal or job duties see themselves as "coaches." These people will be too ready to give you quick-fixes, pep-talks or platitudes which will not be of much help. Anyway, what you really need is to get your own concerns out into words, not someone's advice. The latter may be very useful later but not now. Get someone, to repeat, who is a good, attentive, receptive listener, someone who can keep still.

Thus the irony of a self help book on dilemmas, distress and stress is to suggest, first of all, that you go to another person! People are so very important in anyone's troubles. Two phrases which summarize the first step are: FEEL IT! GET IT OUT!

Taking this first step of finding a listening friend is harder for some persons in a crisis than for others. So we should add one more question to ask ourselves: How do I feel about seeking help? We are very accustomed in our society to expect we should be able to handle all of our own problems that seeking help, particularly for "self-sufficient" individuals, comes hard or is embarrassing. In some ways men are especially prone to this self expectation. Seeking help goes counter to any number of cultural sayings: "Pull yourself together"; "In our family we handle our own problems"; "A real man pulls himself up by his own bootstraps," and so on.

We will seek an expert in economics, in legal matters, in nutrition and most everywhere else, but we assume that everyone is his own best expert in personal feelings, social skills, family conflicts, self-defeating attitudes and the like which bring so much misery into our lives. Why should we not need help in crises, in conflicts and frustrations which are experienced in our family life, in our needs and other people, in our work, our motivations, and strong bonds with others?

Are personal needs and feelings not less complicated than our finances, our legal limits, our dietary requirements?; they are only less obvious. Expert help is as much needed in our crisis, if not more, than any other important area of life.If we need reassurance about seeking help in crisis; if cultural truisms about being independent haunt us and make us feel guilty, we should remind ourselves of other truisms: no man is an island; no one can carry his or her burden alone all the time; there are limits and breaking points to everyone. At that moment, we need the help of others — even professional others at times.

STEP TWO: GET A HANDLE ON THE PROBLEM

Once you have found someone to whom you can talk and get your "story" out, the next thing you need to do is come as close as you can to grasping what the real problem is. It means you have to see what is really upsetting you. Sometimes this is easy and sometimes it is very difficult. I call this "Getting a Handle."

I'm Doing My Best . . . But It Isn't Enough

A first thing you can do is rank order all those things which are part of your distressing dilemma. For example, Ned is a young man whose girlfriend just broke off his engagement, he is flunking a night course he is taking, he is spending a lot of extra time on his job because he fears being laid off for not meeting his quota in selling electronic equipment. He put a priority on these problems and found his threat of job loss was the heaviest worry bothering him. While his love relationship and academic failure were distressful, it became clear that what was central to him at this time was his job aspirations. Next in his importance was the failure of his love relationship, and lastly, his failure at school. He felt better by just putting his finger on the problem, by just understanding what it was that was so bothersome.

A second thing one can do is a strategy close to what many people often do. Since a dilemma involves making a decision, people often put down the pros and cons of each decision. Irving Janis has come up with a very useful tool, a balance sheet, which is shown on the next page, Figure 2-1. At first it will look very familiar but on inspection, it contains some very new and helpful ways of sorting out the choices one has in a dilemma.

In brief, the balance sheet is applied like this. You make such a sheet for each option, say of staying together in a difficult marriage or of separating, or staying at your present job or leaving. But each option gets its own balance sheet. Then you write down the pros and cons which are tangible for yourself. Then you write down the pros and cons (e.g. of staying put) for important other people, such as your family. All of this you have probably done in one form or another.

The new wrinkle comes in the third section: Reasons for self-approval or disapproval. Here you can ask yourself such questions as these:

*Do I feel good about myself for this option?
*Is this consistent with my favorite picture of myself, of the kind of person I would like to be?
*Is this option consistent with my ethical/religious values?

Figure 2-1
The Balance Sheet Procedure

FIGURE 20. The balance sheet grid.
Alternative # _____

	Positive Anticipations +	Negative Anticipations -
1. Tangible gains + and losses - for SELF		
2. Tangible gains + and losses - for OTHERS		
3. Self-approval + or self-disapproval -		
4. Social approval + or disapproval -		

*When I write down three things I most want to become, these are

_____, _____, _____,

(e.g. strong, intimate, considerate, ambitious, consistent, etc.)

Is this option promoting these things in me personally?

Finally, you ask what kind of approval or disapproval you are going to get from others who are important to you.

The special feature of the third and fourth sections is that it brings into our dilemma our values and priorities of life; these are often omitted in the usual balance sheet which people make. But these are important considerations to "getting a handle" on one's dilemma. We can live with or are haunted by a dilemma in which our own cherished ideas are violated. If we violate them, the dilemma comes back in the form of guilt or shame or sadness.

A third way to get a "handle" on what our problem is is to ask which of the following statements are true of me?

*I am in a stew because something is in the way to my getting what I aim for: my boss, a supervisor, a spouse or family member, federal regulation; or something else is in the way but it is a lack: not enough training for a job, not enough social skill to handle a difficulty, not enough guidance or skill, or insufficient money.

*I am in a stew because I cannot decide what I most want to do; my dilemma is due to indecisiveness — not of knowing what I want though being barred from it. I just cannot make up my mind. I guess I want my cake and to eat it too.

The third way of coming to grips with what your real problem is can be summarized this way:

A. I am behind a barrier, or
B. I am in a bind.

Chances are you will find your dilemma can be put into one of these two statements. In Chapter Four, these ways of getting a grip on one's problem will be discussed in great detail. If you can answer the question (a bind or a barrier?) you will go a long way toward solving your own dilemma.

STEP THREE: GET RID OF RIGIDITY

Your greatest need in the distress of a dilemma is to be flexible, and your greatest enemy is to become mentally and physically rigid. Consider how this problem arises in these people.

Joseph was facing bankruptcy with his business failing and high interest rates. He kept saying over and over to himself and others? "I'm going to lose my store... I'm going to lose it... I'm going to lose it." This is all he could think of. Mentally he kept running over the same thoughts. It was stereotyped thinking: the same thing is done over and over though nothing improved.

Russ, mentioned in the last chapter, kept saying: "How embarrassing that I didn't get the promotion.... What a shame. ... How awful.... How disgraceful." The same thought kept dominating his thoughts. Likewise Pat and Helen continued to have the same fights, to use the same unproductive ways of communicating; they reverted to the earlier, first learned ways of talking to each other about their grievances and differences. And so it is with everyone in stress: the enemy is rigidity.

What has happened to these people in a dilemma is a self-inflicted hazard, though it is understandable. Each one narrows his or her focus and limits the view of what can be done. The result is that all these people lose or limit their ability to turn to new alternatives and this is the principal reason why they say, "I do not know what else to do." They have done their best, with what we have called their Emergency Skills and they get stuck there, not able to use Adaptive Coping (such as the Three Beacons, to be discussed in the next chapter). They are stuck and frozen in a single way to handle their dilemma.

One of the first things we notice about being in a crisis is that we get tense. We get to feeling uptight or "tied in knots." The third step can be best explained by running with the image of being knotted up. Imagine, if you please, that you are trying to secure a boat with a storm raging. You have to tie up the boat or it will be swept away, capsized and be destroyed. Now suppose in the last few days, as part of your new ownership of that boat, you have taken some special instruc-

I'm Doing My Best . . . But It Isn't Enough

tions on boatmanship and have been taught some new knots, unlike those you usually tie. The new knots are better, yet with the storm battering you are very likely to tie the rope in the same old way.

The point of this imaginary threat to your boat is that in a crisis we tend to rely on first learned ways of coping with problems. In this sense, we resort to the old ways of handling problems and some of them may be "primitive" in that the old skills do not work well. Still, we use the same old ways over and over when we are in a crisis.

At the same time, the knot tying image holds another, very positive clue: *the second most basic need, after being listened to, in a time of crisis is a search for a way to do something.* In a crisis and in any form of stress, much of our behavior is a search for any way to act. The next chapter on this need for *our* initiative. We most need some way to come on with independent action, some solution or control of our own. A person who is passive simply feeds the pain of vulnerability and increases the crisis. The greatest relief in a crisis is to *do* something. The worse reponses for persons in even the most severe stresses, such as concentration camps and physical illness, is to give up and do nothing, to relinquish control of what they can *do*.

So if you are in a crisis, hold on to the image of being "tied in knots." It is a reminder both of what you most need, which is to take some action, and also of your own biggest barrier: returning to primitive, out-dated and unproductive ways of solving the problem.

The practical step here is to do something which will rid ourselves of using old, ineffective solutions. The practical thing here is anything which will not make us so *rigid*. Being tied up in knots and getting tense, in muscles or emotions, is our enemy; getting rigid is self-defeating. The basic law of stress is that *the more severe the crisis, the more tense and rigid throughout our whole personality we tend to become.* We have to counter this tendancy.

Fortunately there are many practical steps we can take toward rigidness. These are the strategies offered in the abundant number of self-help books available. They offer methods of *relaxation*.

We should not be deceived by the meaning of "relaxation." This is a special set of exercises which cure rigidity. Relaxation in this sense means something very different from the person who says, "I relax by reading a good book, or going to a favorite lounge and have a drink with friends, or by a ride in the country, or going to the movies, etc." These are *not* the forms of relaxation which will help a person cope much better with stress; they may help some when used together with what we suggest here, but mainly as supplements.

Figure 2-2

Start your relaxation by getting as comfortable as you can. Find a chair or couch which is comfortable and where you can elevate your feet to be level with your body. Do not cross your legs or arms because this cuts off circulation. Sitting in your chair the first thing to do is to take a deep breath, filling up your lungs as much as you can and hold it for about three to five seconds; now let the air out slowly. Repeat this exercise of deep breathing one more time. Begin to feel yourself relaxing more and more. Feel relaxation taking over your body.

Muscle Relaxation. Once you have taken some deep breaths, the next stage involves relaxing your muscles. It goes like this. Stick out your right arm, make a fist until you feel tension in your hand. Hold the hand in a fist, continuing to feel the tension for seven to ten seconds. Now let your fist relax, and notice the sensation. Your hand is likely to have tingling sensations. This tingling is the first of three signs of relaxation. It is curious tension. So it is also with knowing any mental state of peace and calm: it often comes after knowing some form of tension such as anxiety or restlessness. Now repeat the exercise of clinching your fist and holding it for seven seconds. Again, let your hand relax and focus more closely on the sensations in your hand. You will notice three kinds of sensations: *tingling, warmth* and *heaviness*. These are all signs that your hand is relaxing. Notice these qualities in your various muscles as we now proceed through various parts of

I'm Doing My Best . . . But It Isn't Enough **45**

your body. The procedure is the same: do the tension-followed-by-relaxation two times for each of the following muscles.

*Now put your left arm out and make a fist. Relax. Again make a fist and relax.

*Make a fist in both hands at once. Relax, noticing the sensations. Repeat making fists of both hands.

*Continue with each of your arm muscles: your forceps & biceps.

*Relax your shoulders and neck muscles by lifting your shoulders as far upward as you can. Hold the pose as you feel the tension in your shoulders and neck. Let go and relax. You will probably now feel some very soothing relaxation in your shoulders. Repeat the experience of your shoulders and neck.

*Now begin to relax your face muscles: bite down on your teeth and hold it until you here feel the tension. Relax. Repeat. Now, smile broadly, as wide a smile as you can until there is tension in your facial muscles. Relax and then repeat. Now close your eyes as tightly as you can, feel tension and then relax. Repeat. Make a frown, as big a frown as you can so that your forehead begins to feel tense, hold the frown. Now relax and repeat it.

*Now let the relaxation which is in your hands and arms and shoulders and face spread throughout your entire body. Begin to feel the calmness and ease spread throughout your entire being.

*Talk to yourself inwardly, saying, "I'm relaxing more and more. I am more comfortable and relaxed, comfortable and relaxed."

*Now continue to relax the muscles of your torso and legs: first your chest, then your stomach and abdomen, then your thighs, calves, ankles and feet. Finish by tensing and relaxing your toes.

*You are now feeling relaxed in all the muscles of your body. Reflect upon your state of relaxation, noticing how good you feel. Now find a word you would like to use to describe this state of relaxation. Make it your own special word, the one which for you best expresses how good you feel. It could be, "tranquil," "serene," "calm," "at ease," "restful" or any other which you like. It is your own special word. Say your word over and over again, "I'm serene (or whatever)."

*You may find that later, in the middle of the day when you are doing your regular activities, you can pause for a moment say "your word" and something like the state of relaxation you just experienced will reutrn! It is that kind of control which the mind can have over your body.

Let me add that neither I nor anyone else is claiming that your anxiety and tension is totally cured by such a simple set of exercises of your muscles. However, one of the places where anxiety does register is in your muscles, and this is a very simple, modest way of reducing that tension and that expression of anxiety. And it may work more than you ever expect — if you have never tried it before.

☆☆☆

The importance of getting rid of rigidity through relaxation probably cannot be emphasized enough. If you now refer to Figure 2-2 you can experience a form of relaxation most adaptable to your stress. Please try it. As I indicated earlier, one of the greatest boons to live at a time of the "stress popularity" is the wealth of methods for relaxation. I have referred to those as the Short Order Solutions — S.O.S.

At the same time, it is of utmost importance to see relaxation in its proper perspective, as having a very specific function or aim. *Relaxation is helpful to you only to the extent that it reduces rigidity in coping with distress of dilemmas.* I would like to highlight this function with what may seem a fanciful suggestion.

"GO FLY A KITE"

I mean this as a very serious suggestion. All sorts of re-newed abilities come to a person who goes out and literally flies a kite. I recall on a warm, clear day seeing a man

I'm Doing My Best... But It Isn't Enough

in his fifties doing literally this. No children around as an "excuse for this thoroughly childlike (not childish) activity." As I passed he grinned broadly, as if for a moment being self-conscious. Then with a gleam in his eye he returned his full attention to the soaring object.

This is a thoroughly fine form of relaxation, but it is even more a symbol of what the third step should be, to cope with rigidity. Flying a kite may be a symbol of any form of regaining flexibility. First, regaining flexibility requires you to do something actively, and to give your full attention to something other than what you have been doing or thinking about — over and over.

Secondly, flying a kite is like any other form of reducing rigidity in giving you an entirely new perspective. Any effort at flexibility should take you from a stooped shoulder position which you have while working and worrying; looking upward you see things in a new way. Thirdly, with a new perspective you get ideas you have not had for a long time. Solutions to problems you once dealt with will return to you, as perhaps at no other time. You have the best opportunity to regain your strengths which will be discussed in the next step.

Fourthly, flying a kite, as any beneficial form of regaining flexibility does this: *prevents us from being a chronic, unproductive "worrier."* The worrier is a person who never quite does what he or she is doing. That is, worriers never fully attend to what is presently at hand. When they are at today's task, they absent-mindedly drift into worrying about demands of tomorrow. Then when tomorrow comes, instead of concentrating on that task, their mind goes back to thinking about the previous day — and the regrets of not attending to yesterday. In a word, worriers never fully attend to what is presently facing them; this is a main source of their rigidity. Their worries do not get fewer; rather, with each day one more worry simply gets poured into the confused mass they already have. Worriers have a pattern of living which invites more fears, inhales more threats. It is a rigid-producing cycle, all because a person does not fully attend to one problem at a time.

What do worriers have to do with flying a kite? They do the opposite, which lessens their flexibility. A flier of kites —

and any form of active relaxation — leaves off one concern to fully attend to another. He also changes his perspective, uplifts his views. But the important role of active relaxation is also to *detach a person from that which is fatiguing him.*

In a word, to handle your distressing dilemma it is of utmost importance that you detach yourself from the dilemma. This is the key to ridding yourself of rigidity and regaining flexibility. Kite-flying may be a model for you to do that, even if not at something literal to do.

STEP FOUR: REGAIN YOUR STRENGTHS

If you are in the distress of a dilemma, you feel weakened.

If you are in a crisis, the next thing for you to do is to take stock of your resoures. After you have talked to a friend, and have a handle on adapting well, after you have set the stage for more flexibility by doing some relaxation exercises then you are now ready to call upon your strengths and resources, and to use them in a new way.

Let us see why this is so important. The central feature or inner experience of this crisis is the hurt, even the emotional pain. This is the very reason why one of our first steps is to air our feelings. We discover that the core of this pain will often be that we feel vulnerable or helpless. We may call this being "anxious," which is rather like a blow to your head. We react with. "What's happening?" We are dazed and knocked off-center.

What we are probably asking in our crisis, maybe without being able to put our finger on it, is: "Can I do anything about this? Is this problem able to be undone or reversed?" And we very likely have given a doubtful reply in the middle of the crisis? "Probably not."

If you are in a crisis, hard questions are actually being put to you. Such as, "Am I strong enough, skilled enough to deal with this? And, beyond myself, is there someone I can or want to turn to for help?" So we need some assurance that we can answer "yes" to these questions, but this is not always easy because of our state of mind and emotions.

The hardest thing to remember to do in a crisis is to recall our strengths. In a crisis we have "selective recall:" we select to remember mainly our weaknesses or failures.

I'm Doing My Best... But It Isn't Enough

There are three kinds of resources you should know about to prepare for upcoming stresses particular to you. You will need to ask yourself about these resources in these three questions:

1) Resources in yourself: What skills, strengths, abilities within yourself can you rely upon?
2) Resources in other people: Whom can you turn to and rely upon?
3) Resources in your social community: What agencies and professional sources of support are there for me to turn to for help?

You can get a picture of these resources by imagining them as three circles surrounding you, as indicated in Figure 2-3. The second and third circles expand further and take in more territory.

In the outer circle are resources in your civic community at large and we have just spoken of these. They range from personal services to public agencies and programs. You should check out as many of these resources as possible as relevant to your upcoming stress.

The second circle is closer to home, as it were. These are the most important resources of *other people*, particularly those in the same boat. You may have noticed the following experiences:

*People going through a divorce find it helpful to be with others going through the same experience.

*People who have problems with drinking or other addictions find it helpful to be with others like themselves.

*Labor union leaders who are overworked profit by having "bull sessions" with others in the same situation.

*People who are injured gain much strength by sharing with others with similar handicaps.

Figure 2-3

RESOURCES

I need to know and use my strengths or resources...

- ...IN CIVIC COMMUNITY
- ...IN FRIENDS
- ...IN SELF

I'm Doing My Best . . . But It Isn't Enough

It is like the saying goes: "We didn't come over in the same ship, but we are all in the same boat." Nothing helps you in stress so much as being with people who also are going through the same stress, or who have gone through it.

This second resource has profound reason behind it — in your needs. You have a need you should recognize in stress: that need is to be with others not only for support, reassurance, and for other obvious help, but the need to be with others goes deeper as part of your own resourcefulness. The reason for wanting to get together is often something people are not aware of, but it is a very powerful need of resourcefulness. It is this need: *to know yourself*.

Much of the time you will be able to understand yourself only through being with other people. You get your feelings. But you also compare yourself with them. You have in your stress the need to understand your opinions, your coping abilities, and your feelings. These things you can best understand by being with other people and comparing your opinions, abilities and feelings with others.

The third resource is in yourself, as the circle indicates. I earlier quoted the quip that "there are three things a person must do alone: die, testify, and putt." Handling stress hopefully is not one of them, except after one has fully used other resources to bolster one's own resources.

Yet in some sense, stresses must be handled ultimately by ourselves. There are limits to the resources others can be to us. We must bring our own best selves, talents, abilities and strengths to that stress. Only when we ultimately handle the stress ourselves can we expect to come out of the stress better and stronger. The entire next chapter will be devoted to enlarging on this resource, your Self, while practically handling your stresses.

There are a number of ways to shore up one's strengths when we are in a crisis. We can begin with some ways to improve our *self-image*, that is our view of our strengths. A first strategy is very simple but extremely effective. First, write a list of nine things you like about yourself (e.g. helpful to children, good conversationalist, good organizer, good cook, and so forth). Then take a set of ten index cards and write one of your positive features on each card. Carry the cards with you through the day and at a pre-arranged time (e.g. *before* a coffee break, at lunch, starting your car, smoking a cigarette, etc.) read one of the cards; consider reading a positive thing about yourself as a ticket you "must" have before treating yourself.

A second thing to do is make a list of things you are *not* good at, such as swimming, telling jokes, math. Then get together with a friend and run down the list saying, "I am not a good joke teller (or whatever) and I am a worthwhile person.[1] This is more important than it may first appear; we often tend to equate a limitation with being an unworthy person in a very complete way — which, if pushed, we know is not true. You might know someone who does not view him or herself as being a good conversationalist and then talk of him/herself as being totally worthless. This exercise prevents one from falling into such a trap.

STEP FIVE: GET A PLAN

Once you have admitted your feelings, explored them by talking to a good listener, and got a handle on the main issues of your dilemma, and then attained some flexibility and regained some self-confidence — after these steps, it is time to take some action. The fifth step is to *do* something, with a *plan*.

This step is the hardest one to state briefly. Often it comes down to making a decision. Often it means deciding: (a) to stop doing something you have been doing; (b) to resume doing something you once did but have no longer been practicing; (c) to carry out some plan you have been thinking about but never put into motion; (d) to try something new which you have never tried before; and, usually you will want to decide, (e) what you want to continue to do that you have been doing. Stress expert Donald Tubesing has summarized these five kinds of decisions: deciding to DROP, RETAIN, PLAN, RESUME, or DARE. Figure 2-4 gives a helpful form to use in making some decisions which he suggests for stress and which may be helpful for distressing dilemmas as well.

---

[1]. Suggested by Dov Elkins, *Teaching People To Love Themselves* (Growth Associates, 1978)

I'm Doing My Best . . . But It Isn't Enough 53

Figure 2-4

A. FILL IN THE BLANKS:
1. MAYBE I DON'T NEED TO _____ ANYMORE
2. MAYBE I DO NEED TO _____ SOME MORE _____
3. MAYBE I NEED TO _____ SOME TIME SOON
4. MAYBE I NEED TO _____ ONCE AGAIN
5. MAYBE I NEED TO _____ SOMETIMES

B. THE POINT IS, FOR EACH DECISION:
1. WHAT YOU WOULD LIKE TO CHANGE   DROP
2. WHAT YOU WANT TO HANG ON TO   RETAIN
3. WHAT ARE YOUR FUTURE GOALS   PLAN
4. RECALL A RESOURCE FROM THE PAST   RESUME
5. AN AREA WHERE YOU NEED MORE FLEXIBILITY   DARE

_____

DRPRD

C. TWO EXAMPLES OF EACH DECISION:
1. I don't need to be such a perfect housekeeper anymore
   I don't need to worry so much about my work anymore if I'm doing my best
2. I do need to develop some more interests outside the house
   I do need to spend more time with Billy and Bob
3. I need to find a part-time job
   I need to look into opening a business of my own sometime
4. I need to go camping with Billy and Bob once again
   I need to take long walks once again
5. I need to hug them without warning
   I need to bring Betty long stemmed roses sometimes

I. REORGANIZE II. CHANGE THE SCENE
III. CHANGE YOUR MIND IV. BUILD UP YOUR STRENGTH.

The crucial thing in this final step is to take some action. It will not be sufficient to deal with our crisis by merely getting an "insight" — which then is not acted upon. Step Five is a reminder that a crisis is not a purely mental affair. A crisis is an emotional and physical shock; it is also a call for action. I think we all need to be reminded of what Robert White called the "potential for action."

> We have for a long time been heavily concerned with how people feel, not so much with what they do. It has been our faith that if people could be made to feel right inside, to experience trust... then only could we expect their behavior to change. So we have been tempted to concentrate on these inner states, trying to influence them directly through the power of insight and the efficacy of a relationship. Yet increasingly we have been confronted by the painful fact that this method of getting at the roots of the difficulty is, after all, something short of a startling success... There must be a new sensitivity to *potentialities for action*. (*Coping and Adaptation*, edited by Coelho et al, Basic Books, 1974, p. 66)

Everyday life has *action* as the key way of adapting to difficulties. In a problem we first and last are searching for a way to act.

No one is quite the same after a crisis, mainly because of what s/he has learned to *do*. A crisis, as a turning point for better or worse, may trigger a new set of actions to overcome it successfully. Or when the crisis is not dealt with adequately, what is triggered are some actions which leave us more in pain, more confused, more disheartened.

The final outcome of a crisis is that we turn to one of the following states of action, or lack thereof:
*FIGHT
*FLIGHT
*FREEZE

We will see these in all their forms in the next chapter. The account for our coming out of the crisis or stress better than, worse than, or as good as, we went into it.

But for now, suppose you conclude this chapter in a

practical way. Try asking yourself the questions in figure 2-5. This will probably help you to see what you are presently doing and (to take you some steps further) what you might now try. One has to *learn* in handling crisis, stress and distress. That is, one has to see different ways of responding which are more effective than one is trying — and put these new ways into action. Consider the questions in figure 2-5 as something of a "spot check" on your present and possible coping steps. It is a checklist which summarizes this chapter.

Figure 2-5

CHECK LIST FOR FIRST COPING ACTIONS

Now we have a picture of what our experience is and what the crisis is, let us check on ourselves to see what we have been doing. The following questions will be helpful.

A. What Am I Doing Now?

1. What familiar ways have I chosen to deal with the problem? Are they working now? The fact that I am in a crisis suggests they are self-defeating for the present problem, or at least they are not effective.

2. In a crisis what I really need is a way to act. Have I acted, or have I mainly just worried and "stewed" about the problem?

3. In a crisis, while I am attempting to cope, it will be important for me to retain some personal control. Am I trying to cope by turning over the responsibility totally to someone else (e.g. parent, friend, counselor, teacher)?

4. At the same time, I will probably need other people when in this crisis, not to turn over total responsibility to them, but to share responsible efforts with them. Can I find someone who will cooperate with me in working on a solution, at least by talking with him or her and coming up with plans together?

B. What Might I Begin To Do?

    1. Can I find a friend to talk to, someone with whom I can really GET IT OUT?

    2. How can I GET A HANDLE on the crisis? That is, get a good understanding of the problem, by seeking more information, while keeping my own balance and control of the situation.

    3. Have I made efforts to GET RID OF RIGIDITY? Have I gotten less uptight and tense which is a barrier to good, flexible coping?

    4. Have I SHORED UP MY STRENGTHS? Am I in touch with resources within myself as well as people I can draw upton to cope well with the problem?

    5. Have I MADE A PLAN, to do something rather than passively stew, or "awfulize" or think that an "insight" solves the difficulty?

Chapter Three

From Groping to Coping — by Three SOS Beacons

TWO TYPES OF GROPING

This is a chapter where Short Order Solutions (SOS) take center stage. But before we get to them you need to recall how you came to experience being in your distressful dilemma, not knowing where to turn. You came to the point when it seemed that you were simply "groping around."

You can either grope or cope. While we have made the point that getting a handle on the structure of the problem is a start to the solution, it is not always obvious that a person might do from there. A person can proceed by trial and error, groping from one effort to another.

GROPING IN TWO LEVELS

Consider Pat and Helen, who are in the distress of the decision of whether or not to divorce. They feel much agony and confusion. Pat sees himself as being the main part of the problem; he has always been more attached to his work than to a commitment and sees himself as being a "rolling stone," afraid of deep and prolonged relationship. He even sees himself as being a wanderer in his work, moving from one company to another though remaining in the same role as purchasing agent. Helen also has a career and now has a job offer which would take her to Europe. A deadline on her acceptance of the job put both in the distress of having to make a decision. They have no children, and the main problem is Pat's resolving of his own conflict of wants: to become more involved in the relationship or not.

This couple reminds one that in a distress, when stress includes a problem to be solved, there is a great need to see the difference between *one's reaction* to pressure, and *and efforts to cope* with the dilemma.

In a distress we have to solve a dilemma. This calls upon our skills. First, persons use routine or "ordinary" skills and if these fail then they try "emergency" skills. Emergency skills are higher level efforts, sort of shifting into another gear. If we return to Pat and Helen we notice that they first talked about their growing separateness, his lack of involvement. Nothing changed with these ordinary efforts at communication. Then they resorted to a special meeting to really "clear the air" and get down to the basics of their problem. They used the best communication skills they knew, tried to be patient and understanding. Still, they began to call each other names, impute selfish motives to one another and ended in a yelling match. Their "emergency" skills really consisted of accusations and name-calling.

When emergency skills fail you, you are in a dilemma. You have done your best but it is not enough. You experience the pressure and tension of stress, but this has now turned into distress, for you are asking, "What can I do?" Distress requires another level of skills, such as abilities to make decisions, formulating some plans or taking some actions. Unfortunately, these decision-making skills may be beyond a person at the time of his/her distress.

When a person is distressed s/he *copes*. That is, s/he does not quite know what to do, but s/he does the best s/he can, often by trial and error to come up with some sort of solution. Commonly, what we call "getting experience" is coping. It may be the coping with something pleasantly and simply new, like skiing or photography — that's a good sort of getting experience. But it may also be at something now, pressurized and terribly important — that's the distressful kind of getting experience.

What we are going to be talking about is *coping* in distress. And we always need to be aware that there is coping and then there is coping. As we mentioned in Chapter One, not all efforts at coping are equally effective. A person can emerge from a dilemma in one of three ways: as well as one went into the dilemma, or worse than before, or, if we are either lucky or skilled we can surface from our dilemma better than we went into it. The last is the attempt of what I will now suggest. I will suggest some strategies which are found for *effective* coping, whereas the first two outcomes are often the result of groping.

EFFECTIVE COPING: THREE BEACONS FOR SOS RESPONSES

There are three "beacons" or guidelines a person should keep in mind while trying to cope with a dilemma. They are the first basic strategies for handling any dilemma where one is unsure about what to do. While they are not final solutions to distressing dilemmas, they do prepare for solutions. In a way they enable a person to pull together much of what s/he can do to ready him/herself for solutions which satisfy.

Robert White has provided us with the "three beacons", though he did not call them such. White suggests that when you try to cope with a situation which is both unknown and important you need to *adapt*. And to adapt you need to do three things along the way: 1) You need to hold to as much control of your situation for your own freedom of action; 2) you need to ensure your own peace of mind and inner harmony as much as you can; and 3) you need to keep a search going for new facts, opinions and options.

I would like to come right to the point about the "three beacons" or adaptive coping strategies and give some practical guidelines. Then I will give some explanation on these three very important guidelines for coping which are really effective and adaptive and distressing dilemma.

The first beacon includes some suggestions for tempering your *experience* of the distress, the stressful part of pressure and tension. And so it helps you with the first face of your distress, your personal discomfort. The second beacon helps you with both your personal discomfort and also enables you to look at the second face of your distress: your *dilemma* to be solved. The third beacon helps you to begin focusing on your dilemma with the first step for real effective coping.

Some Practical Guidelines

BEACON I. REGAIN YOUR BALANCE AND SELF-COMPOSURE: KEEP YOUR COOL

*Avoid awful-izing such as saying "It's horrible; I can't stand it; it's too terrible." These statements aggravate your emotional state and are not true unless you are being tortured to death.

*Also avoid programming your self-image with thoughts as, "Always" and "Nevers". For example, "I always get the short end of the stick: I never do anything right; I've always had trouble in personal relationships."

*Recall your good decisions. Make a list of your strengths, at least nine of them; then put one on each of nine index cards and carry these around and read one of them throughout the day; add a tenth blank card and later put an additional strength on that blank card.

*Talking to a friend will help you regain your self-composure. In addition to getting your feelings out, the friend may help you identify your good decisions and strengths.

*Take a break, such as a luncheon moment in a mall or a drive in a peaceful country side, to get some perspective and away from the problem. This is not avoiding the problem when done for a short time but rather a strategic retreat.

*A sense of humor is a clear way to get perspective. Try to get some comic relief through a book or magazine; even better, by coming up with an observation of your own while in the mall or talking with a friend.

*Do some daily exercises, to stir up your body chemicals and "shake up your mental cobwebs." Jogging or cycling or swimming or a good brisk walk restores balance by invigorating a person.

*Self-composure and balance is particularly gained by exercises in active relaxation, such as in Chapter Two and are available in many self help books.

I'm Doing My Best ... But It Isn't Enough

BEACON II. KEEP AS MUCH CONTROL OF YOUR CHOICES AS YOU CAN

*Remember, we control our own thoughts and feelings, except when being physically attacked.

*Admit to your own feelings. Say as much, for example, "I am frustrated. I feel threatened, worried, defeated, unsure, etc."

*Don't run away into drugs which are a cop-out on stresses.

*You can find your own control is helped by finding supportive persons: those who do not take away your responsibility but who support you in your own decisions.

*But get a wide variety of people to support you: do not depend on "strokes" from just one circle of people or from a clique or limited bias.

*Live by your own standards. Make up your own mind what these are. Make decisions by what *you* feel when at all possible.

*Gain independance from whose who frequently try to control you. Gain this freedom, however, without a lot of putdowns of them; that is, without blaming them, devaluating them or ridiculing them.

*Be action oriented: see your life as calling for actions, your actions. Problems are something you *do* something about, rather than worry and stew about.

*Make some plans. Have some goals, even if they are incomplete or vague. But try to make them as specific as possible.

BEACON III. KEEP YOUR SEARCH FOR SOLUTIONS GOING

*Keep an open mind. Do not give up too soon nor hide your head in the sand. Do not isolate yourself from others, particularly those persons who may have gone through the same dilemma.

*Do not assume you know all there is to know about a problem. For example, if yours is the distress of an illness, try to find out as much as you can about the condition.

*Your biggest enemy in a dilemma is your own rigidity or inflexibility. Among the structures of distresses we have talked about is this inner source of frustration which is a personal attitude of solving problems in the same, unchanging way. This is so important that it needs to be returned to later in more detail.

*Try a technique "So What If." One thought that goes often through one's mind in a distressing dilemma is, "What if..." "What if I get demoted? What if my best friend does not like what I did? What if I get divorced?" Take this thought one step further and add the word, *"So"*: "So what if..." This changes the whole thought, so that you look ahead to real, life consequences of the dilemma. Will you die? Be a beggar on the streets? Be an outcast with no friends at all? The worst calamities are those that never happen.

*Do anything to look at likely consequences.

*Look more closely at your own wants and values. "Value clarification" exercises are available and very helpful.

*At the same time, try to keep the new information at a comfortable rate, at an incoming flow that you can manage. Do not let anyone flood you with great amounts of facts, statistics, diverse opinions.

*You are not the first one to experience your problem, however unique are some of the parts of your situation. Assume that these *are* solutions though you have not found them. They may not be the most comfortable or easy to arrive at but there is always reason for hope.

Commentary of the Three Beacons

ON REGAINING YOUR SELF-COMPOSURE

Your first need in a dilemma is to keep (or regain) your self-composure. This is the first mark which will prevent groping and ensure effective coping. You will need some sort of inner harmony or organization. A dilemma brings on such feelings of distress that a person immediately feels confused and filled with worry. It's almost as if a person were knocked off balance or "out of kilter." Your self-composure is a way of getting your balance back. Young people have come up with an expression today which beautifully summarizes what we most need, first of all, in a dilemma. They say, *"Be cool."*

If our youths suggest we be cool, they are not, of course, supporting air-conditioners. They are offering a suggestion which, having stuck for over a decade, is one of our few reminders of something else: "Keep your presence of mind." *Cool.* is a pithy tribute to the ability to have self-composure when things get roughest; to have self-command, when demands are greatest; to have self-control, when our most sensitive rights are threatened. "Cool, man, cool" — the accuracy of the phrase is alarming.

The reminder is much needed. If we reflect on past stresses and distresses, we probably will be able to recall that this inner sense of organization and harmony was most strongly affected. It is found to be most seriously disrupted in three distressing states: fear, shame and guilt (which we will discuss in Chapter Six). Sometimes after a distress, however, we forget just how disorganized we were. This forgetfulness is one of the carry-overs of being in distress. And so we need the reminder of our youths.

In the distress of a dilemma, everyone needs the beacon of regaining one's inner balance and organization. The man who sees his small business collapsing with continual losses, few sales and pessimistic barometers of the economy is "disturbed" or thrown off-balance, disorganized. A child who is tearful due to being discredited or filled with fear is also disorganized and off-balance. Both need their feelings and self-image restored while working through the distress of a dilemma.

Of all the forms of upset or unbalance we can experience in a dilemma, there is one which is most damaging. That one is a disorganization which is most severe in our *self-image.* "No adaptive strategy that is careless of self-esteem is likely to be any good," says Robert White. For a person to effectively cope, the essential need is to regain and preserve self-esteem.

What is this self-esteem? Everyone talks about it, but sometimes it is hard to pin down when you want to build it up. Here is how I define it. *Self esteem is our image of our own patterns and habits.* Each person defines him or herself in terms of behavior patterns, whether s/he is nervous or relaxed, powerful or weak, passive or active, and so on. Look at Figure 3-1 for further examples.

In a dilemma you are very likely to see yourself as being on the negative end of the scale. You probably will see yourself as nervous, weak, passive, vulnerable, too trusting and so forth. To regain your balance in the distress of a dilemma you will need to recall and consciously cultivate these habits or traits you like in yourself. *These habits are your self-esteem,* but they are questioned in a time of being distressed.

In a dilemma you begin to doubt yourself. In hard financial times a salesperson is most pained by wondering if he or she has "lost it", that is, the ability to sell. In times of a divorce, one woman began to look back to see all her habits as failures: her ways of dealing with her spouse, her abilities to be an independent person with her own career and/or interests. The positive resolution of her dilemma came first as she was able to gain her self-composure on her own image of habits and life patterns. She gained inner balance by developing habits in two areas: she focused on new skills of "letting go" of an old relationship; she worked her roles as a person, a worker, a woman, a sexual partner and a social being. She changed her self image about her behavior patterns and this restored her inner balance and self-composure.

A person in a dilemma is first of all threatened by his/her behavior habits, some of which are related to one's self-image and self-worth. If a person is to resolve a dilemma in a helpful way, s/he must improve his/her behavior patterns —

I'm Doing My Best ... But It Isn't Enough 65

FIGURE 3-1

SELF-ESTEEM EXERCISE

Rate yourself on the following list of terms. First put an **I** in the appropriate blank indicating how you would like to be ideally. After completing all the items, begin the list again. This time put an **R** in the appropriate blank indicating how you think you really are. After you have rated your ideal self, compare the two. You may want to talk to others to see how their ratings compare.

1. Attractive	Unattractive
2. Intelligent	Unintelligent
3. Weak	Strong
4. Passive	Active
5. Fair	Unfair
6. Kind	Unkind
7. Quiet	Loud
8. Introverted	Extroverted
9. Nervous	Relaxed
10. Liberal	Conservative
11. Happy	Sad
12. Boastful	Humble
13. Controlled	Uncontrolled
14. Vulnerable	Invulnerable
15. Excited	Calm
16. Sexy	Unsexy
17. Trusting	Untrusting
18. Powerful	Weak
19. Conforming	Independent
20. Sensitive	Insensitive

Quoted from Tubbs, *Systems Approach to Small Groups.* (Random House, 1st. edition) or sometimes just recall the good ones she has had all along. Enlarging, improving, and developing good behavior habits are the best way of improving one's self-image. And this is how you know you are coming out of a dilemma better than you went into it: your self-defining habits have changed for the better. Your prized habits are confirmed and developed.

On the other hand, an unsuccessful dealing with a dilemma ends in greater upsettedness of self-esteem and one's self-defining habits. Poor outcomes in dilemmas leave a person more upset and unbalanced because s/he sees his or her ways of dealing with matters not only poor but unimproved — and so s/he feels worse about him/herself. To return to a person with the effects of a divorce, for example, the person can come out of it worse than before. S/he can think less of his/her ability to be open in helpful ways, or his/her skills of letting go, or his or her habitual manner of conducting him/herself as a separate individual.

Furthermore, unsuccessful outcomes are noted for the way a person holds *rigidly* to habits that do not work. Such poor outcomes are found in people who rigidly use the same old tactics: they run away from problems, or they get aggressive, or they sulk in alcohol, or become less likely to live alone so that they get caught up in a whirl of activities. But the key point is that they rigidly hold onto old ways, their lack of flexibility in learning new ways when old ways don't work.

As a result of rigidly holding onto old, unworking ways, a person feels worse about him/herself. His/her self-esteem is lowered. His/her self-composure and inner harmony are lessened and s/he ends up experiencing more anxiety, depression, guilt and other upsetting emotional moods.

So, your first step in going from groping to effective coping is to "keep your cool." That is, regain the inner harmony and balance which comes from knowing your self-worth. Recall your good habitual patterns. This will give you self-composure. And, when you find some real lacks, become flexible to learn new skills and new ways to handle problems. Do not be rigid or inflexible, above all. Rigidity is the sign of low self-esteem and being upset.

ON KEEPING AS MUCH CONTROL AS YOU CAN

The point of this "beacon" can be seen in a young woman, Gina, who found herself so distressed that in her office, she found herself breaking into tears before her fellow workers. Her dilemma had nothing to do with her job but rather her personal social life. Two years earlier she had been involved with a man and had become pregnant. He shortly moved to another city but with no acknowkledgement of the child. Gina later miscarried and as time wore on found it easier to put the whole relationship behind her. Then one day the man reappeared into her life and called Gina to ask if he could see her. Indeed, he became rather insistent.

Gina was in a dilemma. She was torn between seeing the man, since she still had fond feelings toward him, and telling him not to call. Upon advice she came to see what bothered her most was not being in control of her situation. I suggested she set out the terms of their seeing one another. She decided she would tell him she would see him once every three weeks, and if she felt comfortable later then she might see him more. But she let the man know that *she*, Gina, would be in charge of where the relationship might now go. Gina felt this was exactly what she needed. Her distress dissipated and she confidently proceeded with her life, though the man did not think enough of her to continue the relationship for long. She knew that it was just as well that she was without him in her life.

As with Gina, so with anyone in a severe distress a major need is to keep as much control as possible: to keep the intitiative in one's own ballpark, so to speak. It serves the very important place of preserving one's self-respect to one's autonomy. Nothing preserves our self-esteem so clearly as for us to experience ourselves as protecting our own rights.

The symbol of keeping this control is seen when a person is not "conned." A person is handling stress when s/he makes a move on his/her own terms — not someone else's as when s/he is not suckered in by false claims of deadlines into buying somethng or, when s/he does not try to meet the arbitrarily imposed deadlines of doing what he/she has chosen for her/himself to do — and prefers to do.

A healthy mark of good decision-makers is to be resistive and even stubborn toward attempts of others to deprive them of their own freedom. It is healthy to want your decision to be your own, and to spontaneously react against anyone who would deprive you of your own choice. You see it in children even. It is all the more healthy in adults. And in times of distress, it is essential for making a decision which ultimately will satisfy you most.

It is curious perhaps, but we want this independence even when we want to talk with a friend about our dilemma. What we want in that friend is not advice but someone to listen. People rarely want to turn over their problem to another, but rather to turn it over in their own mind — by talking about it. We want them, by listening, to help us come to a good solution. No one should expect to have a friend or even a counselor solve his/her own problem for him/her.

You have a need to show yourself the respect of being your own person, retaining ultimate choice in your own hands. Respect that need.

So you may have to delay or hesitate in making the decision. You may want to even, for a time, withdraw from what is distressing you. That is perfectly appropriate. Possibly by talking to a friend s/he does offer a suggestion that seems helpful. Give yourself time to think about it, to make it your own, to take what parts you feel comfortable with and to cut out what you don't like.

The second beacon is effective coping, rather than groping, is to feel that you have some part in handling the dilemma. That is an important part in being adaptive to difficult problems. It does not mean that you do the whole thing, only that you have an important role in the solution. It certainly does not negate what was said about needing people in a dilemma. It simply means that you are going to cope best with a dilemma when you feel you have some *active* part in it.

You have a very profound need to retain or regain your own sense of autonomy or healthy independence. And nothing preserves your self-esteem (spoken of as the first beacon) so much as for you to experience being "in charge" in some way.

ON KEEPING YOUR SEARCH FOR SOLUTIONS GOING

The third beacon for effectively coping with your dilemma is the reminder to continue getting as much information as you can. Keep your options open. What is it about effective coping, that this should be so important as to be a "beacon"? I think the answer can be found in this old saying:

> Half the troubles in this life can be traced to saying "yes" to quick and not saying "no" soon enough.
> (Josh Billings)

Probably the greatest tendency in a dilemma is to say "yes" too soon and so to close down our options. After all, when stress has become distress we are impatient for an answer. So we do not want to keep the search going. We will be satisfied with what looks remotely like a solution. Any solution will do.

On the other hand, an equally strong temptation (which stops the search) is to flatly give up. Some persons in dilemmas have a temptation to see matters hopeless too soon to think that what has been achieved by *their* "regular" and "emergency" efforts (as we described these earlier in this chapter) is all that can be done. This is not usually the case.

More often than not there are solutions and strategies available beyond what you have thought of. It is important that you keep your search going in spite of feeling, "I've tried everything and nothing works." Remind yourself that it's simply "nothing *you've* tried works."

So this is a major beacon in dealing with dilemmas precisely because of most people putting self-imposed barriers to seeking solutions: the barrier of impatience and that of hopelessness which is premature. But "Keep The Search Going" is a valuable motto for other reasons.

Suppose we look at a few facts. Surgical patients who are given advance information about upcoming operations, including how serious they are, recuperate better than persons given no such advance knowledge. Persons with illness such as diabetes adapt better and more effectively when they carry out a search for as much information as possible. Persons with a major life transition, such as career change, going to college, or being relocated, all adapt better when they carry out an ongoing search for information.

Information itself seems to be helpful to people, it has an "innoculating" effect on patients, a reassuring effect on persons confused and a hopeful effect for those who have come to think there is no hope. Information itself if, if you will, therapeutic. This is still another reason why, though you have tried everything and nothing seems to work, you should *Keep The Search Going.*

This is so important that it leads into the major, proven way of really good adapting and effective coping. That single most important style is through *vigilence*. Most poor ways of dealing with dilemmas are in some form lacking this single quality. Poor coping, or groping, seems to be more like inertia, avoidance, blaming, procrastination and the like. So important is this that in Chapter Five we will go into much detail about making a Vigilant Search for the solution of your dilemma.

What it comes to is that a person in a distress immediately experiences a major need: to get a "map" of his/her surroundings or his/her options. You see this in any adult in a new situation which calls for action: he or she first steps back and asks him/herself, "What is this anyway?" S/he is caught in the very natural posture of clearing what s/he expects of him/herself and what other people expect of him/her. S/he is asking, "What are the cues and guidelines for action?" The same behavior is seen in children on their first day of school; they are hesitant, timid but searching, reserved but trying to understand what their options are.

The scanning of one's world is a very urgent need in times of confusion; it is a necessity one should not forget when in distress. The whole point of distress is that one's world is clouded with ambiguity. The main difficulty in a dilemma is that one does not know what to do or where to turn. To Keep The Search Going is a major beacon of effective coping.

One practical suggestion remains about this search for information: *keep the rate of information at a comfortable pace.* This means you should both be open to information, as I have already suggested, and it also means you should avoid an "information overload." There comes a time when you do need to temporarily shut down the number of facts or opinions, so that you can sift through their merits. Do not allow yourself to be overwhelmed by advice about your dilemma, such as an illness, the job market, the end of a relationship.

The point is very much identical to that of Beacon Two: keep in charge. Here it means: take your time and give yourself time to think through your options. Do not put unnecessary deadlines and time pressures on yourself. Keep thinking and searching at a rate which is comfortable to you.

SUMMARY

The efforts to deal with your own personal dilemma can be summarized in your own choice: to grope or to effectively cope. You already are using two levels of skills in dealing with your dilemma. There is, first, your regular and habitual way of dealing with conflict or frustration. If you find these do not work, then you start to apply your own emergency skills which can be in forms of aggression, anger, insistent demands, clearer social skills, calling on others to help, and so forth.

But suppose you still reach the point, "I've tried my best but it still isn't enough." Then you can grope by doing nothing about your state of upsettedness, or turn the decision over to others or to fate, or give up. Or you can cope with the first effective beacons to guide you: regaining your self-composure and inner balance, regain as much initiative and personal control of the situation as you can, and keep the search going for alternatives. In the first instance of healthy coping you are softening the subjective experience of your distress (its first head). In the second instance you are setting the foundation for dealing with the problem to be solved (the second head), and in the third instance you are taking the first steps in keeping your energies focused on the problem to be solved.

Chapter Four

Getting a Hold On Your Problem

Start this chapter by answering the questions on Figure 4-1. This is a way of "jumping in feet first," to get a hold of your problem.

What I hope you have gained so far is some understanding of your situation when you, facing a personal dilemma, say, "I've done my best but it is not enough." Let us reduce your difficulty to a couple of facts.

FACT ONE OF YOUR DISTRESS

The first fact about your distress is the two-headed nature of your difficulty, as you have seen in Chapter One. You know that personal dilemmas are stressful but they are also more than that. You now that your distress has a two-headed monster you must deal with. First there are your *reactions* to the problem (the wrinkles of stress, as it were). Secondly, you also have a problem to be solved, a decision to be made (when stress becomes distress). Both faces of your dilemma need solutions.

Fact one says that some stresses go beyond pressure and tension — the usual way stress is spoken of today in popular circles. Some stresses become *distress* by the very fact of having a seemingly unsolvable problem or of being incapable of a satisfying solution. They bring on the feelng that what you are doing is not enough. But — what else can you do?

FIGURE 4-1

QUESTIONS TO ASK YOURSELF
TO FIND A HANDLE TO YOUR DILEMMA

1. My dilemma: does it make me feel like:
    A. I am up against a brick wall, being frustrated by an obstacle outside myself? Or,
    B. I am being pulled apart, drawn in separate directions by conflicting desires?
2. Is my distress mainly due to:
    A. Being up against forces or persons outside my control? Or,
    B. Being indecisive, vacillating within myself and unable to choose?
3. Is my dilemma due to being unclear about what I most deeply want or wish for?
4. Is my dilemma really a conflict between two equally attractive choices which, however, are incompatable (e.g. two jobs, loving partners, etc.)?
5. Or, is my dilemma really a conflict between choices of all which are undesirable ("between a rock and a hard place")?
6. Or, am I in conflict because what I am struggling for is such a "mixed bag" of pros and cons that I cannot decide if it is a good choice?

NOW READ ON .... TO HELP

FACT TWO: CONFUSION

Now we come to "Fact Two" which means that the primary experience of being in distress is that one is *confused*. In facing the two-headed monster one does not know what to do and so is bewildered about what the solution might be. Dealing with this confusion is what we are about in this chapter.

When you are confused in your distress, the real difficulty is that you are facing a conflict, and in order to get out of that confusion you have to see the conflict and resolve it. For example, here is the confusion of a person who had gone through a divorce. He was forced to acknowledge that what he *said* he wanted in a relationship and what he *really* wanted were two different things.

> *I said I wanted a woman who was interesting as a person, yet I still viewed women as sex objects and second-class citizens. They were primarily to listen to my problems and to take to bed.
>
> *I said I wanted a woman to view me with no illusory expectations, but what I really wanted was a woman who would buy my own illusions about myself.
>
> *I said I wanted an open relationship of shared feelings, but I continued to assume I knew what a woman was thinking or feeling without bothering to ask her. She had to live up to my own fantasies; never mind what she was really like.
>
> *I said I was ready for a mature relationship between two adults, but what I really wanted was someone to take care of me. I was confusing a home-cooked meal with love.
>
> (Mel Krantzler in *Creative Divorce*)

There are all sorts of conflicts in every kind of distress. In some ways it is the conflicts which make the difficulties seem so insolvable. One of the biggest kinds of conflicts is our own motives, values or desires. Thus we may want to be better liked at work but also aim at being a domineering person. In our lives we may both want freedom and also the values of deep, enduring commitment.

It is no surprise that we are conflicted and therefore confused in our personal difficulties. Society does not always help us to be clear in making up our minds. Here are a few examples of how we grow up with motives in conflict. Society says:

*This is a world in which it is "every man for himself and the devil takes the hindmost."
But: no man lives to himself alone; you should love your neighbor as yourself; we should all work together cooperatively.

*Hard work and thrift are signs of sound character; they are the dependable roads to success.
But: the smart people know how to make money and go places without working.

*Doing your own job well, wherever you are, is more important than trying to make a lot of money.
But: money makes the world go around.

*All men are created equal and free; the democratic style is the best form of social organization ever developed.
But: most people are too shiftless, irresponsible, or dumb to be trusted with handling industrial, social and political problems. Let there be leaders and sheep.

*Honesty is the best policy.
But: there are two kinds of people: the caught and the uncaught. The only thing to avoid is getting caught.

Fact Two says that distress is where all the confusion of motives and wants come home to roost, if you will. Fact Two says to know stress and distress is to be forced into knowing what our values and needs really are. In a distress, we have needs and these are threatened. We have desires and there is a challenge to their satisfaction. We have values and their fulfillment is only through exhausting effort.

In short, we have stress and distress precisely because we have needs, values and motivation. We experience distress because of the stern requirements or tough complications in meeting these needs and values.

For all its hassle, hurt and even pain, a distress has at least this clear benefit: it pushes us to the way to make up our mind about what our needs and values are. There is no dealing with distress without coming to grips about our motives and needs and values. Every solution requires that we deal with our motives. In fact, distress has been described just that way: when adjustment is difficult or impossible but motivation is very high.

There are various kinds of solutions to stress and distress. Some are Short Order Solutions and others are Long Term Solutions. Some require change in our living patterns, others lead us to change our outlooks, and even our eating habits. But whatever the solution, it must start with Fact Two: in a distress we are confused, mentally and emotionally. *The solution must enable us to clear up the confusion by getting a handle on the difficulty.*

A SKILL FOR CONFUSION

I am going to suggest a skill which will enable you to get a handle on most stress situations. As I make this suggestion I think the skill has been described by O. W. Holmes who said, "It's a naive domestic burgandy without any breeding, but I think you'll be amused by its presumption." Why some people will think this skill to be with presumption will be clear momentarily.

Ridding ourselves of the confusion and ambiguity of our stress comes about by asking this question:

Is my stress a conflict or a frustration?

The first skilled question then is this:

*Am I in a bind, or behind a barrier?

*Does my stress present me with choices which are unattainable or incompatible, which then leave me frozen, immobile, undecided? If so, I am in a bind — of a conflict type of stress.

*Or, is my stress due to some barrier or obstacle? Then I am behind a barrier — and this is a frustration type of stress.

DISTRESSES OF CONFLICT

Many stresses involve "conflict," a notion which means both something more and something less than what is ordinarily meant by it. We have spoken of conflict before, but now we must see it with a bit more precision. Conflict, according to Webster's Dictionary, means, "an emotional tension resulting from incompatible inner needs." Conflict stresses are those involving incompatible motives; needs and motives are in opposition. Likewise, our choices or options can be incompatible. There are different forms of conflict, but let us look at one faced by a person called Connie.

> Connie is a young woman going to college while holding a part-time job. She had been dating a fellow worker for about six months when he became outraged at her for talking to another man and slapped as well as verbally abused her then and there, at work. Connie ran out in tears, only to be called later by her boss, saying that both she and her boyfriend had been fired.
> Connie's stress continued as her boyfriend called a few days later, insisting on seeing her. She refused but he persisted in calling. Both Connie's roommate and family were irritated when Connie decided to see her boyfriend. Connie's mother denounced her and her roommate was so infuriated at the boyfriend's calling, that she gave Connie the ultimatum, "Either give him up or move somewhere else."
> Connie felt at the end of her rope. She could not sleep, and wept frequently. With nowhere else to live, when her boyfriend asked her to come and live with him, Connie agreed. She had stress continue, however, for she feared the threat of his being violent toward her. Further, she discovered she was pregnant. She also wanted to return to classes which she had not attended for three weeks.

Connie's stressful situation was being in a conflict; torn between the demands of John and her family as well as her roommate. She felt more and more emotional pain as the demands became clearer, and began her usual way of dealing with the demands of these important persons in her life: by refusing to see him and by attempting to talk with her mother. These efforts failing, she sided with John and left to live with him. This too failed as an emergency strategy to solve the conflict. She might have attempted to flounder with other emergency efforts, either by resigning herself or continuing to fight with John except that she discovered she had an unwanted pregnancy. At this point Connie decided to see a skilled friend, Louise, who had training in helping persons with stress and crises. The first thing Louise noticed about Connie's predicament was that it was a conflict, and so she got a hold on the problem rather quickly.

"Of what practical use is it to know that mine is a conflict stress?"

Finding the structure of a stress is more than of theoretical concern. We have already highlighted that knowing the structure relieves us of confusion. But the structure does more.

The values of seeing the conflict in a stress include: 1) many of our stresses are due to conflicts of motives and needs; 2) dealing with our stresses often include the first step of making up our minds; 3) but most importantly and practically, it is by discovering the structure that we discover ways of solving our stresses. *The structure is the solution,* at least the map to the solution.

The structure of the crisis, once seen, tells us that the solution to many crises and stresses lies in making a *decision*. Knowing what the conflict is in our stress tells us what decisions we have to make, and introduces us to the steps toward decision making.

Every coping action involves a choice, a decision. To make a decision we have to know what our motives, needs, desires are. Every choice in a conflict stress is a choice to reduce incompatibles which are holding us frozen, stymied. Any step in the direction of a conflict stress is in fact a decision; we should be prepared to know what decisions we are making.

STRESS STRUCTURE AND COPING SOLUTIONS

Stress structure is the preparation for decision-making. Let us see this by returning to Connie's stress, which we saw to be of a "To-To Type," she being drawn to meet two

I'm Doing My Best... But It Isn't Enough **79**

incompatible needs. Knowing this structure enables us to know what she can do about her stress.

To help Connie it was decided that the first thing to do was for Louise to encourage her to talk. She asked Connie to talk about four matters:

1) Her perception of the problem.
2) Her feelings about the problem.
3) Her ways of handling previous experiences with conflicts involving her parents.
4) What her supports were: who was there she could turn to: other relatives, friends, school counselor.

After listening to Connie get matters out, Louise went on to help her make some decisions. Making decisions meant coming up with Action Plans.

The Action Plans which Louise worked on with Connie resulted in three steps: First, to have Connie assess her own feelings toward John, as well as her family and following that she was to make a decision on whom to stay with; Second, to talk to her parents explaining the entire situation. If she felt that she leaned toward returning home, she should tell them of this preference to see if they would let her return; Third, she could talk to John and tell him also her preference, whether it was toward him or the family. The options are identified: if he agreed to either of her preferences, the matter would end there and the crisis would be solved; if he became belligerent, she could get a peace bond restraining him from bothering her; if she decided to live with him, they could discuss their mututal feelings toward marriage as well as toward her pregnancy and abortion.

What should be noticed about Connie's conflict is that in arriving at those action plans, there are certain needs which she or anyone in a crisis has. A major need, and it is part of the solution, is that Connie restore matters to her own hands: that is, get some kind of control over the situation. Getting this control is often no easy or quick matter; it is acquired in part by what Louise did for Connie, being a good listener so that Connie could get her feelings out. The next thing which is a step toward regaining control is "getting a handle" on the situation by seeing what her pain was really that of a conflict, being torn by two incompatible forces. This was not only reassuring, but it helped Connie gain some idea of what her action plans should include. The action plans were first to have Connie assess *for herself* what her preferences were, toward John or the family; the other action plans also included her taking the initiative of calling both family and John.

So, regaining some control is one of the biggest needs of a person in a crisis or stress. Another thing required of the person is to keep some self-composure, some sense of balance or equilibrium. This, too, is attained by merely talking matters out; it is also maintained by resting or finding some relaxation; often it may include deliberate skills of relaxation. In particular, efforts to restore one's self-worth will be necessary in most crises and stresses. Thirdly, Connie needed to continue seeking new information: what are her options? Will her family take her back? Will John be prepared to adjust and compromise? What are her own feelings toward pregnancy and abortion?

What tells us that ours is a stress of conflict is the way we seem to be frozen or stalled by our own motives and needs. There is an experience of tension within ourselves which drains our energy. Emotional turmoil mounts because of indecision. Conflict crises are known by these signs: vacillation, hesitancy, mental blocking. Often there is denial and avoidance of efforts to resolve the conflict. If the conflict endures for a lengthy period, fatigue invariably results.

Before we discuss other forms of conflict stress, it should be noticed that the forms of conflict have been very well-defined in psychology. So well that this is the reason for the hesitancy of introducing them here, since claiming this to be a handle on confusion may seem "presumptuous" as mentioned earlier.

But the usefulness of both concepts of conflict and frustration is that they allow us to see the *structure* in every stress. By seeing this structure we clear up our confusion, rid ourselves of disorganization.

Solutions to stress require that we grasp the structure of stresses. In stress we are searching for a way to act; we are in search for a solution. Solutions are the coping. The first coping is to find the structure. Like all coping, finding the structure eases the emotional pain, relieves the ailment, does away with some of the distress, restores our peace of mind, fills us with renewed confidence that there is hope of coming through this stress.

All other solutions wait on our ability to grasp the structure of our stress. We cannot cope further until we grasp the structure: Grasping the structure of stress is to get a handle on what we are experiencing and what the problem is that we must solve. Structure of stresses clears up both sides of stress, the experience and the problem. Structure also very often becomes the guideline for solving the stress.

TYPES OF CONFLICT: BETWEEN ROCKS, HARD PLACES AND DEEP WANTS

Conflict 1. The first type of conflict is what Connie experienced. This conflict is when two incompatible choices attract us. We are drawn to two opposite directions at the same time. We may call this then, a conflict of the To-To variety. Connie was drawn both to please her boyfriend and her parents, but she could not have it both ways under the circumstances. Another example would be of someone in the conflict between two attractive job offers (or more) attractive homes to buy, or apartments to rent.

Conflict 2. Another form of conflict stress is when we are motivated to avoid any of the choices which we have but we *must* choose one. This is the stress between choosing "the lesser evil." *We are between a rock and a hard place.* It is the stress of a man with a serious heart condition who finds it harder and harder to do his work, enjoy his life, on the one hand, and undergoing open-heart surgery to replace a heart valve. Neither prospect is very appealing. The lesser evil must be chosen. This is also the stress of many marriages: to choose between living in an existing marriage which is unsatisfactory or getting a divorce which is undesirable. This form of stress we may call a *From-From* conflict. We are in conflict desiring to move from both options — though we cannot, and this is the threat which produces stress. It is more likely to be the structure of stress than the first type, the To-To conflict.

Conflict 3. This is a form of conflict which puts together needs both to approach and to avoid the same course of action, at the same time. We both want something and do not want it. We literally have "mixed" feelings about an option. This, a *To-From* conflict, is seen in Mara's stress.

> Mara is in a conflict stress in her marriage. She wants to discuss the growing tension and aloofness with her husband. On the other hand, she is afraid to openly bring up these matters because her husband not only refuses to do so, but threatens to kill himself. On one hand, Mara feels the need to find more satisfaction and less pain of tenseness at home; on the other hand, she has the need to avoid "triggering" her husband's suicide.

Mara's stress is due to two incompatible motives; both a desire and a fear are invested in the same course of action. She at once wants to take some step about her marriage and also does not want to. It is a conflict, of the *To-From* variety: torn between the desire to move to a discussion in the family and a fear holding from it.

Mara wants and needs to talk things out with her husband, seemingly a very sensible way to cope with yet another conflict which is interpersonal. At the same time, she fears his reaction, a suicide attempt. Obviously, her natural reluctance to talk with him in his guarded condition is worsened by her *belief* that she is responsible, at least in part, for what he might do. She is not only sensitive to his feelings, but she takes a great deal of responsibility for his behavior, as well as her own.

When Mara sees that the stress is one of conflict, she may be able to begin dealing with the situation, first, by finding a way in which she can resolve the incompatibility in this course of action. Thus she can recognize her needs as sensible and appropriate. Then, she can begin to make such decisions such as: How can I get him to talk? Insisting on going to a marriage counselor, having a friend her husband trusts arbitrate, having a trusted friend support each of them and guide them in constructive sharing.

There are many different ways to solve a marital dispute. But before Mara feels comfortable or even strong enough to attempt any, she will probably have to clear up a very basic question in her own mind: will he really attempt suicide? A still

I'm Doing My Best . . . But It Isn't Enough

more basic question: Am I really responsible for his behavior, if he does attempt this? Or, are there limits to what I am responsible for in anyone else's behavior? She may really have to start her coping by examining these questions and admitting at most a "maybe" to the question (Will he . . .), and a "yes, there are limits" to the second inquiry about her responsibility for what he does.

We cannot stay frozen in a conflict forever. We must resolve it in some way, either to toughen ourselves to stay in an unhealthy relationship, resigning ourselves, or to admit that some situations may be too demanding and intolerable for anyone, and to take some efforts either to improve them or dissolve them. Either way, some *change* has to be made. There must be a change either in ourselves on our part, or a change in the other person: for most unhealthy marriages, the change must be in the *relationship,* with adjustments made by both parties.

Conflict 4. The final form of conflict is the most frequent stress of all. In this type of stress we are facing two or more options, and each has both attractions and repulsions. There are more options than in conflict 3, but each is a "mixed bag." Consider, for example, the stress of Micki, a 19 year old Taiwanese woman in the United States on a visa.

> Micki is under a great deal of stress concerning her decision to marry an American man who has proposed. On the one hand, she feels she does not really love him very much; she also suspects she cares more about a man she knows back in Taiwan; she also does not feel she is mature enough to get married at the present time.
>
> On the other hand, Micki is realistic enough to know that the marriage to the American would give her citizenship status; it would also mean she would live at a higher economic level than is likely in her native country. Micki is torn.

We can all profit from reflecting on her stress, however. Her dilemma helps us to understand matters which are common to many of our stresses. First, Micki sees there is a decision to be made and this decision is the source of all her emotional pain. Second, faced with a decision, Micki has already employed her good judgment to explore, with emergency skills, the pros and cons of each option — most of us do that already in our own stressed decisions. Third, and closely related, most of our decisions are not between clear-cut issues; the options each have merits and disadvantages. Most of life's stresses are filled with multiple plus and minus signs. It is so hard to weigh them out. Fourth, for Micki, as for most of us, a stress pushes us to the wall of our priorities, as it were.

DISTRESSES OF FRUSTRATION

A second structure stress may take is that of frustration — to which you may respond immediately, "Well, of course stress is frustrating!" You know already that the results of stress are aggravating, irritating, hateful, and leave you agitated. But the real meaning of "frustration" as it offers aid to understanding stress is not in these *results* of stress, but in seeing frustration as a cause of stress, and this means frustration is a barrier, an obstacle, an interference.

A Frustration Stress is when some aim or plan or hope has been interferred with — by a barrier. For example, this is the particular stress experience in the employment market: a middle management person in his forties sees that most of the promotions are going to younger persons. There is a prejudice against a forty-five year old worker. And every prejudice, whether of age, sex or ethnic origin, is a barrier and an obstacle.

As with a Conflict Stress, Frustration Stresses always involve our motives or needs. The stress will be greater according to the importance of the motive.

Frustration 1. Teri is a thirty-year-old woman who was helped to see the structure of her stress.

> Teri's stress concerned her fifty-year-old aunt who was suffering an illness. At first diagnosed as having bronchitis and then receiving the letdown that she had brain cancer, Teri's aunt was very depressed and upset. Although the stress lasted over a period of six months, with the family having time to prepare themselves, Teri felt the stress

increasing. Teri particularly experienced stress because, "I don't know how to talk to my aunt. I don't know what to say. She asks, 'Why me?' and I don't know what to say. So I avoid going to the hospital, but I feel terrible about it."

Theresa's stress is a frustration: that is, there is a barrier experienced from a lack of an ability to be able to help her aunt. There is the incapacity to handle an important personal relationship in a manner which is as helpful as Theresa expected.

Notice that this barrier is from *within* Theresa, in contrast to Mary's which had an interference from outside her. Theresa feels at a loss: important to answer not just one big question but two: simply talking to her terminally sick aunt and also answering a specially poignant question: "Why me?"

With the stress defined as a frustration, Theresa can begin her coping. She is reassured in getting at least some grip on the problem, but knows she can begin to deal with the matter. The first thing she might begin to do to remove the barrier is to go to some resources where she can learn to talk to a terminally sick person. Here she will understand what does a person in this condition *want* to talk about? Does she typically want to face the nature of her illness or to avoid it?

Theresa will learn first that there are stages of a dying person's reaction: denial, anger, making compromises, resignation and a degree of comfortableness in living with her condition. Theresa then can find out for herself where her aunt is. She can ask her aunt what her feelings are. One of the first things Theresa is apt to find out is that her aunt probably wants to talk directly and openly about the matter and not to skirt it, or deny it, unless this has been the characteristic of both her aunt and the other relatives. Eventually, however, it is a certainty that her aunt would like to talk about herself and her condition.

In short, Theresa can begin to cope with the first part of her stress of frustration: by learning there are ways to talk to her aunt. As to the second question ("Why me?"), Theresa can begin to cope but it will probably be in a very different way. Once she acknowledges that the stress is due to a barrier, she will have to ask: is this question capable of an answer?

What is the likelihood of any satisfactory answer? Probably she will find there is no likelihood of anyone having such an answer. At least she can start: would the physician know? Clergy? Psychologists or psychiatrists?

All indications are that no one would presume to be able to answer such a question. That being said, there are two options Theresa might explore: first, perhaps the question indicates that her aunt is in her anger stage, does not really expect an answer but needs to get this feeling out; Theresa should talk about it. The other option, if religious views are held by her aunt, might be to pursue the theological view of pain and suffering. That latter could be accomplished by discussing such a book as Harold S. Kushner's *When Bad Things Happen To Good People* (Avon, 1983).

Teri's stress is a reminder to anyone in stress, that some stresses come from barriers *within* themselves. Stress should suggest some soul searching. A person should look closely at himself/herself: his/her talents, training, personality. Some stresses come from being too shy or acquiring a disease. There are other frustrations, coming from barriers outside us, to be sure. But we should perhaps not be too quick to leap at these for explanations until after we have looked at ourselves. Being too quick to see the source of stress as outside us leads to scapegoating, accusing, and blaming others too readily. And these prove to be less healthy means of coping.

Clearly, the sharpest forms of stress include those which take the shape of an illness, such as a heart attack, a crippling disease, or personal injury after an accident.

But there are other examples of Frustration 1: in the stresses of one's career and marriage.

The key to understanding Frustration 1 is in one single word: *Expectation*. Our expectations create the stress.

Frustration stresses are more severe when the barrier is sudden and unexpected. These are the stresses when the reaction is more likely to be hostility or rage.

Frustration 2. The second variety of Frustration Stress is the most obvious of all: the barrier comes from outside ourselves, as is the case with nineteen year old Harry.

> Harry is just out of high school and wants to go to work to earn some money. He wants to be able to

I'm Doing My Best ... But It Isn't Enough

buy some things he has always hoped for. He also wants very badly to be independent and set up his own style of life. But Harry's father has other ideas and insists that he go to college. If Harry does not go directly to college, his father will disinherit him. Harry has always felt like a puppet, feeling that regardless of how hard he tried to make his own decisions, his father really dictated every move. Now, it is happening again. Harry knows that actually he does not have the financial ability to live independently of his parents. Further, Harry has the image of himself as being independent and personally responsible. But his parents would not let him carry out this role.

Harry's stress was one of a frustration: his father's demand presented a barrier to his getting what he wished. It is a barrier which goes beyond simply opposing his desires; his father's dictate was contrary to even Harry's self image and has him seeing himself as a pure puppet, without any control over his own life. This barrier is a frustration which originates outside himself, but enters deeply into his feelings. He had his own plans and his own wishes, but his father stepped in with an obstacle which leaves him, while in stress, unable to move forward.

It is one thing to be deprived, another to have a frustration stress. Being deprived, a person purely without what one might have. It may hurt but efforts have not been taken to get what one wants.

But to have a frustration stress, a person has also been planning, hoping, pursuing. Some effort has been interferred with.

We know we are in a Frustration Stress when, once the barrier has been called to our attention, we continue plugging away.

Once Harry sees the structure of his stress, he will know what he must do to cope: he must somehow remove or "get around" the barrier. If he is skilled enough and his father is open to discussing rationally the matter, he can handle it this way by conflict resolution skills.

Other forms of Frustration 2 come readily to mind when a barrier to any sort of need is placed before us. There are barriers which lead us to feeling, first of all, "lacks": the engergy crisis, decreasing supply of clean water, parks taken away, unemployment. Equally stressful would be a marriage partner who refuses to work at improving the relationship, or policies preventing a persons getting a job promotion. Secondly, there are other barriers which come by way of "excess": pollution, congestion on the highways, or too many stoplights while going to work. Excesses often seem to follow what I call the Law of Cruel Coincidence which runs like this: On that very day when you are most in a hurry, a freight train will cross your road!

As with knowing the conflict structure of Stress, so too with knowing the Frustration Structures, we are then given a start on knowing how to cope. The first thing that having this structure in mind does for us, is to help us know what *not* to do. The first "knee jerk" reaction to frustration stresses is to attack with rage, to get into an argument. A second reaction, also less adaptive, is to repress what we want; a third one is to go back to old needs; a fourth way is to just stagnate. So we can give into 1) aggression, 2) repression, 3) regression, or 4) inertia.

A better way to cope with frustration stress is seen in the clue of our own first behavior of shifting around. We should look for options, keep looking for other solutions, keep an open mind, not close our doors. And this, by the by, is what is also the first step in good decision making which we will take up next in the following chapter. But we should notice again, rigidity is our enemy in coping with stress. Aggression, repression, regression are all forms of rigidity. Being flexible and searching is the better part of coping.

Let us conclude getting a handle by seeing how prone you are to Frustration Stresses. Here is an exercise for you.*

Choose the most appropriate answer for each of the 10 statements below as it usually pertains to you. Place the letter of your response in the space to the left of the question.

---

*Quoted from Girdano and Everly, *Controlling Stress and Tension*. Prentice-Hall, 1979.

I'm Doing My Best . . . But It Isn't Enough **89**

How often do you. . .

____ 1. When I can't do something "my way," I simply adjust to it the easiest way.
    (a) Almost always   (b) Very often
    (c) Seldom   (d) Never

____ 2. I get "upset" when someone in front of me drives slowly.
    (a) Almost always   (b) Very often
    (c) Seldom   (d) Never

____ 3. It bothers me when my plans are dependent upon the actions of others.
    (a) Almost always   (b) Very often
    (c) Seldom   (d) Never

____ 4. Whenever possible, I tend to avoid large crowds
    (a) Almost always   (b) Very often
    (c) Seldom   (d) Never

____ 5. I am uncomfortable having to stand in long lines.
    (a) Almost always   (b) Very often
    (c) Seldom   (d) Never

____ 6. Arguments upset me.
    (a) Almost always   (b) Very often
    (c) Seldom   (d) Never

____ 7. When my plans don't "flow smoothly," I become anxious.
    (a) Almost always   (b) Very often
    (c) Seldom   (d) Never

____ 8. I require a lot of room (space) to live and work in.
    (a) Almost always   (b) Very often
    (c) Seldom   (d) Never

____ 9. When I am busy at some task, I hate to be disturbed.
    (a) Almost always   (b) Very often
    (c) Seldom   (d) Never

____ 10. I believe that "all good things are worth waiting for."
    (a) Almost always   (b) Very often
    (c) Seldom   (d) Never

Scoring: 1 and 10. a=1, b=2, c=3, d=4   Score: _____
    2-9: a=4, b=3, c=2, d=1

    Summarizing frustrational stress, it is found that overcrowding, prejudice and discrimination, socioeconomic elements, and large bureaucratic structures are a few of the elements capable of causing, or at least contributing to, the inhibition of human behavior. Such inhibition is capable of producing psychophysiological stress reactions which are expressed in the forms of anger, aggression, increased sympathetic nervous activity, and an increased incidence of mental trauma.

Having reviewed some of the causes of frustrational stress, go back now and look at Exercise 2, which examined the perception of being frustrated. Statements 1 and 10 show your flexibility and patience. Items 2 through 9 indicate frequent perceptions or feelings of frustration. The highest score possible is 40 and the lowest score is 10. The higher your score, the greater your perception of frustration and the more stressful frustration would appear to be for you. General guidelines are: 26-40 = High frustration / high stress; 20-25 = Moderate frustration / moderate stress; 10-19 = Low frustration / low stress.

SUMMARY

In stress we are disorganized and feel ourselves unbalanced. We can spot our own disorganization in our behavior: we may break into a rage, collapse into tears or resign to lethargy. Or we may show our disorganization by acting at random, attacking the problem in shotgun fashion. Or we may simply do nothing at all and become totally inactive. All of these are forms of disorganization. If permitted to persist, they may become permanent and take on a form of quasi-organization.

Quasi-organizations are signs that we are coming out of stresses weaker, more crippled, less able to cope with future stresses. Quasi-organizations mean we are adopting a life style that is self-defeating and further stresses will leave us more and more defeated.

We must attack disorganization and confusion in every stress solution — long term or short term. To deal with the disorganization we experience in stress we must first get a handle on our stress. That is, we must at the outset get some way to feel control; we must get the feeling of knowing where to start to solve the problem.

Since ambiguity is the shroud that every stress wears, we must do something to strip the stress of that ambiguity. We need a skill which dispells ambiguity which produces our confusion and disorganization. At the same time, this very skill which dispells ambiguity will relieve us of some of the emotional discomfort of pain.

I'm Doing My Best . . . But It Isn't Enough

We need a skill which clarifies our situation, in every stress and each kind of stress. This ability to clarify our stress situation is what I call "getting a handle" on the stress.

In conclusion, some of the stress threats in our life come from barriers and obstacles to our plans or hopes. Knowing what these barriers are the problem enables us a way to plan an "attack" or at least a way of dealing with our stress. We can call stresses with barriers Stresses of Frustration, and get a handle on these difficulties.

There are two forms of barriers, however, and each will require different skills and reactions:

> *THERE ARE BARRIERS WITHIN US: FRUSTRATION STRESS #1
> *THERE ARE ALSO BARRIERS OUTSIDE US: FRUSTRATION STRESS #2

Chapters Seven and Eight will offer practical help for Stresses of Frustration 1; Chapters Nine and Ten will be helpful for Stresses of Frustration #2 as well as those which are a combination.

SUMMARY OF THE SKILL, "GETTING A HANDLE"

One of the first skills that we need to cope with stress is to begin to adapt to the stress *mentally,* to travel the Mental Path of Coping as was indicated in Chapter Four. Travelling that mental path means first of all to get a handle on the problem: find some structure so that we understand the stress better. We can do this by asking:

> Am I in a bind, or behind a barrier? or,
> Am I in a Conflict Stress, or in a Frustration Stress?

The answer to this question is the key to the solution of our stress. Getting this structure clear will provide a clearer "map" to how we might best cope with our stressing threat. There are four types of Conflict Stresses and two types of Frustration Stresses.

Chapter Five

Decisions: on Actions and Attitudes

DECISION MAKING TIME

Your distress is strongly linked to decisions. So it is with most people. A large part of special stresses and distresses today is a clear off-spring of all the decisions which people have to make, plus the special pressures when people make their decisions. In a word, decisions are at the heart of dilemma and distresses.

This chapter is a pivot, with much that has been said so far leading up to the decision making skills to be presented now. Clearly, dilemmas are reduced to making decisons. Equally clear is the fact that distress is a time when stress has raised a decision for you to make — and you don't know what to do. Your regular skills fail, so do your "emergency" skills. You are doing your best but it isn't enough. You try your short-order solutions but they do not help for long. You talk to a receptive supportive friend, you try to relax, regain your strengths: these steps help but you must go further. When you try to get a hold on your problem, seeing it either as a conflict or a frustration, you are preparing your way for making a decision. You are now ready to sharpen your decision making skills.

From here on we will be employing skills in decision making for handling very particular dilemmas. Very recent work on decision making from experts will be of much help as we proceed. Modern improvements on making good decisions will be of great value in helping you overcome your own dilemmas. The material of this pivotal chapter is heavily dependent upon the perceptive and reliable work of Irving Janis and Leon Mann, *Decision Making* (Free Press, 1977). This work is of enormous help in personal decisions.

I'm Doing My Best... But It Isn't Enough

A couple of words of reassurance are in order here. First is the comforting reminder that you come to your distressing decision with some experience. You are not on unfamiliar ground. You have been making decisions as a matter of course all of your life. Decision making is a life-long experience; decisions are routine, some very singular, some are even stimulating and some are terribly worrisome — as in your dilemma. But you are experienced in and familiar with making decisions.

Furthermore, you have been preparing yourself for making better decisions. In a very real sense, the short-order solutions (SOS's, I have called them) are at their best preparations for more quality decisions. Thus relaxation exercises, self-concept building, avoiding the pitfalls of "awfulizing" and all the rest prepare you for sharpening your decision skills.

Nevertheless, even though every person is experienced in making decisions, this does not mean that everyone is equally good at it. Even the preparation of short-order steps does not make all people skilled at making decisions. The very fact that a person says, "I've done my best but it isn't enough," indicates that his or her skills need improving — beyond what experience has taught. "Experience is the best teacher" is counsel often repeated. Is it true? Well, yes, in some. But we each also know many people who do not seem to learn from experiences: they simply seem to make the same mistakes over and over again!

STYLES OF DECISION MAKING

Because a person makes so many decisions today, everyone has developed his/her own style of decision making. You have yours, and now is a good point to find out what style you have promoted in yourself. So, pause and take experience found in Figure 5-1.

FIGURE 5-1

Directions. Below are some statements of different ways of making decisions. Choose the alternative that best summarizes how you generally behave and place your answer in the space provided.

(A) Almost always true (B) Often true
(C) Seldom true (D) Almost never true

___ 1. I tend to act impulsively
___ 2. I tend to get very anxious for an uncomfortable state of indecision to be over.
___ 3. I too easily get confused with the pressure of a deadline.
___ 4. I tend to give myself premature deadlines to make a decision.
___ 5. I tend to "latch on" to the first, earliest option.
___ 6. I tend to avoid making the necessary decision.
___ 7. I tend to blame others for problems before I make a decision.
___ 8. I tend to procrastinate longer than is necessary.
___ 9. I tend to turn to alcohol and other drugs when facing a decision.
___ 10. I often take refuge in sleeping when a decision is facing me.
___ 11. I tend to do a lot of "busy work" when facing a decision, to avoid making it.
___ 12. I tend to exaggerate positive outcomes in making decisions
___ 13. I tend to minimize negative outcomes before making decisions
___ 14. I deny my negative feelings and moods before making a decision.
___ 15. I tend to think outcomes of my decisions won't happen "for a long, long time."

I'm Doing My Best . . . But It Isn't Enough **95**

___ 16. I discount what results the decision may have on people other than myself, but who are important to me.

___ 17. I tend to see myself as a "victim" in decisions, having little control and responsibility for outcomes.

___ 18. I tend to believe the addition search fields not really useful information.

Now add your sore: A =13, B = 2, C = 1, D = 0

Before I tell you exactly what your score means, let me explain something about Decision Styles. Decision-making in distresses begins with knowing how to go about it, and what *not* to do. This means that there are styles of decision making, five of them in fact. One is helpful and the other four will usually be self-defeating. The styles can be summarized by this break-down:

*Helpful style: Vigilant decision making

*Self-defeating styles: Panic
   Inertia
   Unworried Change
   Avoidance

Vigilant Style. A person is vigilant in his/her decision making when three conditions are met. First, s/he is aware of the serious risks in each alternative s/he is considering, and so s/he does experience conflict (remember, experiencing this conflict is the mark of a *good* decision maker!). Secondly the person holds some hope for finding a satisfactory solution to his/her dilemma, so s/he is in some way *optimistic*. Finally, the decision maker believes that there is adequate time to search and to deliberate before a final decision is made.

So vigilance in making a decision requires that you clearly see the risks and are somewhat upset, but that you also have enough self confidence that a solution will be found. In addition, you have given yourself enough time to make a good search and deliberation. Your vigilance, therefore, comes down to experiencing these things in yourself:

WORRY
OPTIMISM
SUFFICIENT TIME

The first, Worry, may come with a feeling of reassurance, of welcome relief that the uncomfortable feeling you have is all right, acceptable, and is in fact the mark of a good decision maker. This very condition of worry will enable you to be aware of the step you are taking, the consequences of what you are choosing, the risks and benefits which will be coming to you as a result of your controlling your life. It is the mark of a good decision maker to worry! If you experience this, then be reassured!

The second, Optimism, is the hope you carry with you that life's problems can come to some sort of solution, not always the ideal solution nor the best arrangements but a solution which you can *accept*. Optimism means having hope, idealism. Optimism means awakening expectations and energy. Optimism does not mean utopian dreams. Optimism means *something can be done* which will satisfy to a degree.

Finally, the feeling that you have time means you can ensure feeling a degree of comfort going through the process. It is the comfort of feeling in control, of having the independence or freedom you like to see in your deliberation. The comfort does not mean that the decision is uncomplicated or easy, nor even that the outcome will be without risks or drawbacks when all is over. The time means that you are able to give unpressured attention to all the things you want to consider *at a pace you can handle*. It is the pace which is somehow confronting — if not easeful.

Self-defeating Styles. If any of these three conditions is not met, you might find yourself in a less than helpful style of solving your dilemma. Perhaps you panic, and do not give yourself enough time. In the questionnaire above, items numbered 1 through 4 were testing just that, a panic style of decision making.

Perhaps you find you do not let the conflict register, that is you are not sufficiently aware of the risks in each choice. This is measured by item five where a person tends not to be sufficiently upset or aware of the risks. His/her style is more inert.

I'm Doing My Best . . . But It Isn't Enough 97

On the other hand, a person may delay making a decision. They procrastinate and put things off. Items 6, 7 and 8 are scored highest when this is the style.

Avoidance is still another self-defeating style of decision making and has at its root a basic pessimism about coming up with a satisfactory solution to a dilemma. Items numbered 9 through 18 are all the ways a person can avoid their dilemma. This is undoubtedly the most widely used method of *not* dealing with a dilemma satisfactorily.

Looking back on Exercise 5-1, an overall score may tell you something valuable about your own style. A total score of 54 to 72 is extremely high, 36-53 is moderately high; 18 to 52 is moderately low; and 0 to 17 is exceptionally low. Either a Moderate High or Extremely High score will suggest that you may want to improve some features of your decision making style.

Decision Know-How

HOW MAJOR DECISIONS START

The first thing which happens to put you in a dilemma is a sudden change of events. You get a piece of news that shocks you, even jolts you: your cash flow is low, the air conditioning motor breaks down, your child is flunking, your spouse is finding it quite a bit harder to live with things being as they are between the two of you, the company is considering laying off workers, and so on. Something new is developing. A decision may have to be made.

Some decisions get started from a sudden jolt much like hearing news from your doctor on results of a test which say you have a heart murmur. Probably more often the "news" is filtering slowly, gradually and you get more aware that something is awry. Your twenty-year-old son has been getting more irascible by the month; it is no shock that he wants to leave home.

Either way, most human beings do not make major decisions until something comes along to change the pace. We usually are content with laissez-faire, continue with matters as they are until rudely awakened with a message: *all may not be well.* That is when we need choice know-how: the skill of making a good decision.

The best skill in decision making is to take matters in stages. These stages, in turn, seem best approached by asking yourself a series of questions about your dilemma. Figure 5-2A is the set of sequenced questions.

Decision know-how involves knowing what steps to take and when to take them; it also entails using a strategy of vigilance and avoiding other strategies, as you have already seen. We'll be using an approach which we have grown accustomed to in these pages, but here we'll provide a structure for taking the right steps in the right steps in the right way. Now see the questions within your steps, Fig. 5-2B.

STEP ONE: GET IT OUT

When the need for a decision dawns, this is usually distressing. You wish you didn't have to make it, but you are becoming more and more uncomfortable with matters as they are. First rule: get it out. As you have seen before, you must put the matter on the table, perhaps to talk with some but at least to spell it out to yourself. Write it down. You'll be tempted to ignore it, not to rock the boat — a temptation to avoid which can plague you throughout the decision steps. But if you do not get it out, this oversight will come back to haunt you.

One thing which getting it out does for you is awaken Vigilance in you. What it saves you from is the first pitfall of decision-making, *Inertia*. Some people never become good decision makers because they are seemingly fixed, unshakeable, and shun any threat of danger off with a bland, "No Problem!" And the problem proceeds to run over them!

It is better for you to get out in the open what a risk is; it will alert you that something has to be done. Your first motto may be to take as your own the poster which says:

DO SOMETHING! LEAD, FOLLOW,
OR GET OUT OF THE WAY!

The first vigilant step is to be alerted. The first mistake you can make is to "stand pat," and conduct business as usual when it is not.

I'm Doing My Best . . . But It Isn't Enough

Figure 5-2A:

QUESTIONS IN A DECISION

1) HOW MUCH TIME DO I HAVE?
2) WHAT ARE MY CHOICES AS I SEE THEM NOW?
4) HAVE I BACKED AWAY TEMPORARILY TO GET SOME PERSPECTIVE? NOW THEN, WHAT DO I REALLY WANT TO BRING ABOUT BY THIS DECISION?
5) CAN I COME UP WITH A NEW, AS YET UNCONSIDERED OPTION?
6) NOW WHICH OPTION APPEARS TO BE THE BEST ONE TO CHOOSE?
7) WHAT ACTIONS SHALL I TAKE, WHICH ATTITUDES RE-SHAPE?
8) AM I NOW READY TO ANNOUNCE MY DECISION?

A second pitfall which getting it out will help you avoid is a too ready movement to change: to go in for the surgery, to firmly and quietly leave your job for another, to walk away from your spouse. In some dilemmas such an action may seem preposterous (such as leaving one's spouse or job), but in others it it all too likely: this is how people buy lemons in cars and stocks that fall through the bottom.

A pattern of vigilant decision making becomes clear in this first step: there is a value and indeed a necessity of being *concerned*. I will go further and put the matter bluntly: it is the mark of a good decision maker to WORRY! A moderate degree of worry will be your best friend through your decision in a dilemma. It may sound like you're replacing your distress with worrisomeness, and so it is. But to worry is better. It will get you out of your predicament when rightly used.

What worry will do for you is prevent you from too soon closing down your decision process. Worry keeps the process going. Someone has said (TRW advertisement)

DECISIONS ARE EASY IF YOU NO IT ALL.
IT'S EASY TO SAY "NO" TO A NEW IDEA.
YOU JUST HAVE TO SEE THE PROBLEMS.
SAYING "YES" IS HARDER. YOU HAVE TO
SEE THE POSSIBILITIES. (Fortune 5/14/84)

Figure 5-2B:

THE QUESTIONS WITHIN A FIVE STEP PLAN

STEP ONE: GET IT OUT

STEP TWO: GET A HANDLE ON THE PROBLEM

    1) HOW MUCH TIME DO I HAVE?

    2) WHAT ARE MY CHOICES AS I SEE THEM NOW?

    3) WHAT ARE THE PROS AND CONS OF EACH ALTERNATIVE?

STEP THREE: GET RID OF RIGIDITY

    4) CAN I BACK OFF TO GET SOME PERSPECTIVE AND REST?

    5) NOW THEN, JUST WHAT DO I WANT MOST FROM THIS DECISION?

STEP FOUR: GAIN YOUR STRENGTH

    6) CAN I FIND ONE NEW OPTION I DID NOT SEE BEFORE?

STEP FIVE: MAKE A PLAN

    7) IS ONE OPTION NOW SUPERIOR?

    8) WHAT ACTIONS WILL I TAKE, WHAT ATTITUDES RE-SHAPE?

    9) AM I READY TO DECLARE MY DECISION TO OTHERS, WITH SELF APPROVAL AND SUPPORT FROM IMPORTANT OTHERS?

STEP TWO: GET A HANDLE

In making a decision, this step means asking two questions and the first is:

(1) How much time do I have to decide?

Notice what *time* has to do with good decision making skills. It has been said that we human beings are "time-binding animals" and indeed we are. The simple notion of how much time we have will often determine which strategy we use in making our decision. Notice for example:

1) If there is plenty of time, plus hope for successful solution and awareness of serious risks, we will be vigilant, discriminating and open-minded;

2) If there is absolutely minimum time, plus hope of successful solution and awareness of serious risks, we will be hypervigilant and panic;

3) If there is lots of time, even with serious loss possible and hope, we will procrastinate;

4) If there is little time, awareness of losses and chance for good outcome to come from someone else, we will shift responsibility;

5) If there is little time, no chance to shift responsibilty and big risks, we will tend to use avoidance strategies.

The second question to ask yourself in making your decision also helps you to get a hold of the problem:

(2) What are the alternative courses of action available to me as I see them now?

Do I see only two alternatives, sort of a go-no situation? Stay at home or leave? Keep my car or buy a new one? Go to the college of my choice or not? Redecorate our home or leave as is? Stay at my present job or leave? Stay married or divorce? And so on.

In your own dilemma you will probably see more than two paths, and that is all to the good. Few choices will end with a solution based on simple-minded either/or thinking. You have probably shown your good potential for a decision if you have come up with three options; if your first survey of alternatives brings to light four or more options then compliment yourself! You have the makings of an excellent decision maker.

Good decision making is the knack of generating as many possibilities as possible. For this you need time and the feeling of being secure in what you know, in what *you* feel are your options, and in exploring your own life which you control.

But here is a moment to notice another general rule to guide you through your decision. *Good decisions go from the NOW to the NEW.* Begin unravelling your dilemma with what you are aware of *NOW*. Don't rush headlong into new facts which will leave you in a state of disorganization.

Going from the Now to the New preserves you from some of the pitfalls of less desirable styles. It prevents you from feeling you are *panicking,* the basic feature of which is the feeling of being out of control. Going from the Now to the New sets matters in stages and you can go from one stage to the other when *you* are ready. As you have seen in every form of adapting (Chapter Four), you need to keep as much control in your own hands as possible.

By this question, "What are my alternatives?", you will also be preventing yourself from shifting responsibility (an avoidance). You are maintaining the attitude that the choice and the alternatives are indeed "mine." You will be owning the problem, and after all, don't you really prefer to keep the decision yours in the long run?

(3) What are the pros and cons of each option?

Now you come to the question which is so obvious to you. We all take this step so it is hardly surprising. Yet it is good to get to this question here, after we have surveyed the previous matters. You are now in a better position to see what the pros and cons are: the rewards and costs, the possibilities and risks.

Nevertheless, I am going to suggest that there are some surprising new nuances in this step. While you intuitively consider the pros and cons of your alternatives (in buying an oven, divorcing, taking a job, going to a school) you may not consider all of the *types* of pluses and minuses. Virtually everyone profits by some special features in the balance sheet introduced.

	Positive Anticipations +	Negative Anticipations -
1. Tangible gains + and losses - for SELF		
2. Tangible gains + and losses - for OTHERS		
3. Self-approval + or self-disapproval -		
4. Social approval + or disapproval -		

In brief, the balance sheet is applied like this. You can make such a sheet for each option, say of staying together in a difficult marriage or of separating; or staying at your present job or leaving. But each option gets its own balance sheet. Then your write down the pros and cons which are tangible for yourself. Then you write down the pros and cons (e.g., of saying put) for important other people, such as your family. All of this you have probably done in one form or another.

The new wrinkle comes in the third section? Reasons for self-approval or disapproval. Here you can ask yourself such questions as these:

* Do I feel good about myself for this option?
* Is this consistent with my favorite picture of myself, of the kind of person I would like to be?
* Is this option consistent with my ethical/religious values?
* When I write down three things I most want to become, these are....

STEP THREE: GET RID OF RIGIDITY

The time has come to get rid of some narrow channeling of thoughts. Here the step is to gain perspective and there seems no better way to begin this step than by "getting away" from the matter for a time. It could be called a "strategic retreat." To withdraw from your worrying vigilance is enormously helpful. It should not be confused with *procrastination* or *avoidance*, for these are pitfalls which a temporary time away from the problem will prevent. This recommendation is precisely to get away *for a limited time.* Give yourself permission to ease up, back off, take advantage of the "time" you are alloting yourself.

Perhaps the most important thing which will happen to you in this strategic retreat is that you will be able to focus on the next question.

(4) Have I backed away temporarily to get perspective? Now then, what am I really wanting to bring about in this decision?

You've had your aims and objectives up to this point; they were veiled in answering your balance sheet. But this is the time and place to bring your deepest wants and cherished hopes out into the open. This is the time to put your decision and options into perspective. Consider these examples of summarizing perspectives:

"In deciding whether to leave home or not, what I really want is my own independence."

I'm Doing My Best... But It Isn't Enough

"In staying with this job, though other options seem to offer more tangible advantage than this does, I really want the camaraderie of the people I now know."

"In deciding on whether or not to divorce, what surfaces as my keenest desire is the chance to have my own 'space' in which to try out things."

"As I look at the two ways to support myself through college, I most cherish the status that is going to be coming."

This is soul searching time. It is the time when we really get down to the heart of the matter. This is what will lay our soul bare.

It sometimes comes as a surprise how, after a person has made out three or four balance sheets the person will end up choosing the option which has fewer pluses and more minuses, excluding that option which on the basis of most plus entries seemed more plausible. Here we have the reason why. Good decisions which satisfy are those which are based, not on the quantity of entries but on the quality. The quality of entries are those which are more likely to bring about our deepest wants. This helps you to answer this question?

What few outcomes do I cherish most?

STEP FOUR: STRENGTHEN YOURSELF

Now is the time to take the step from the now, into a new alternative. It brings you to the fifth question:

(5) Can I come up with a new, as yet unconsidered option?

To answer this in a vigilant way, it might be good to take some new steps. I would suggest these: (1) talk to two people you know about how they would approach this problem; (2) read some discussion of the dilemma, perhaps in a magazine article; (3) pay a visit to some expert resource place (career guidance centers, apartment finder, women's group concerned with the effects of separation, professional therapist, etc.)

STEP FIVE: FOLLOW A PLAN

Now you should be ready to ask the next question:

(6) Which option now appears the best one to take?

By this time you know what your alternatives are, you have weighed the pros and cons, you have singled out important outcomes you want from the decision, and you have searched at your own pace for new solutions. You should be ready to identify which way you want to go. You have done all you can do to make it *your* decision, indeed, your best decision in the circumstances. And you have preserved your own best self and preferred values in the choice.

This brings you to the next question:

(7) What actions will I take, what attitudes to re-shape?

Your solution to your dilemma will definitely include taking actions: to quit your job, to decide to leave your present city, to open your own business, to stay in or leave your marriage, and so on. The actions which are part of your plan are usually so much a part of your decision as to be inseparable and clear. I say clear, not always easy.

You have perhaps heard of the different kinds of reaction to stress and distress:

*FIGHT
*FLIGHT
*FREEZE

It does appear true in distress that people wil either lash out in an attack (if not rage), or they will retreat from what they are suffering, or they will become immobilized — being fixed and unable to react at all. This three part breakdown of options is a handy way to begin knowing one's options in making a plan and acting on it.

The Fight-Flight-Freeze options are different "routes," if you please that a person can take to deal with a dilemma. Let us pursue this image further and say that there are "maps" we can make for our plan out of a dilemma. We can map our way and which route we take will result in our coming up with a solution which is real and satisfying or coming up with a solution which is a dead-end. A choice of one's route is therefore crucial, a real turning point.

I'm Doing My Best . . . But It Isn't Enough

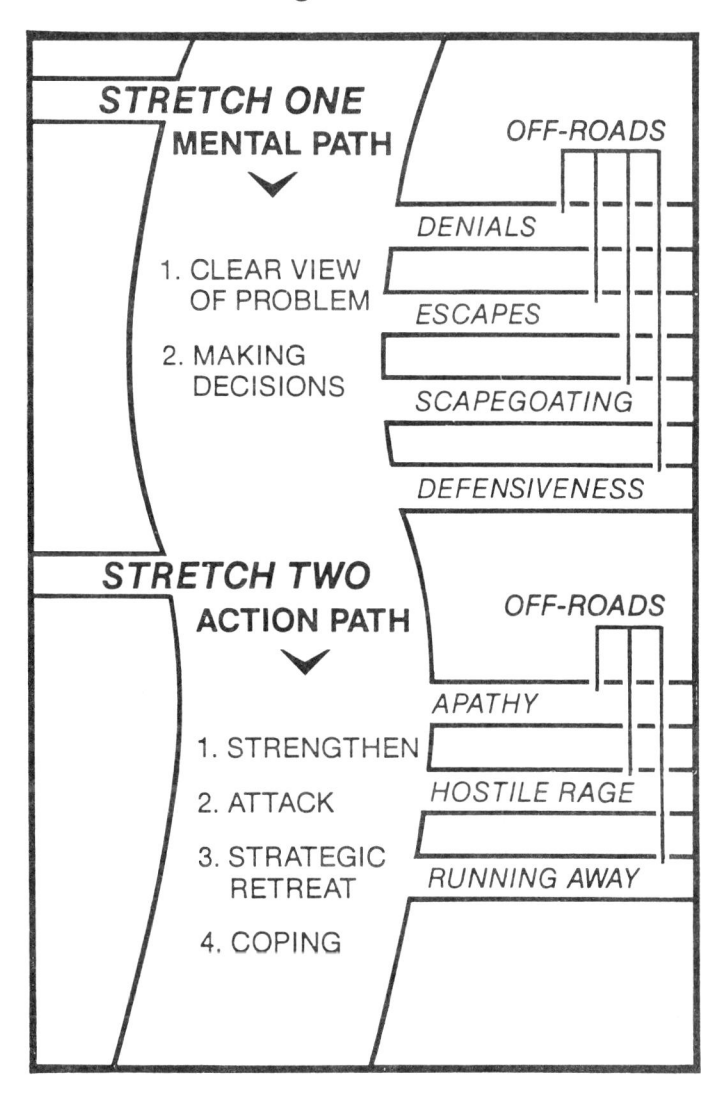

Figure 5-3

STRETCH ONE
MENTAL PATH

1. CLEAR VIEW OF PROBLEM
2. MAKING DECISIONS

OFF-ROADS
- DENIALS
- ESCAPES
- SCAPEGOATING
- DEFENSIVENESS

STRETCH TWO
ACTION PATH

1. STRENGTHEN
2. ATTACK
3. STRATEGIC RETREAT
4. COPING

OFF-ROADS
- APATHY
- HOSTILE RAGE
- RUNNING AWAY

Suppose you put your plan visually in the form of just such a map as in Figure 5-3. Your plan will entail strengthening or readying yourself for action, directly confronting it, taking some steps of appropriately withdrawing from some issues and declaring your decision to others. In the same vein, there are possible detours you will want to avoid: apathetic inertia, uncontrolled rage, and attempts to run away from the matter.

There is, however, another side to your decision plan. In addition to the actions you can take there are your attitudes to reshape. You must be alert to your mental steps just as you are careful about your behavioral actions.

It is these attitude steps which really result in your *long-term solution* to your dilemma. It is these which really tell you when you have come out of your dilemma better than before — or worse. We have been dealing with the mental aspects of coping with your dilemma for most of this chapter. The "styles" of decision making are basically attitudes: from vigilance, to panic to inertia and avoidance. Decisions are a question of attitude.

In a sense the first reaction to your dilemma and distress is mental. Your choice is *how* you cope mentally, not whether you cope mentally. Your first solution is in your head, and it is there also that your final solution must be. To try to cope by actions only, without a mental reaction, is like jumping into your car and racing off wildly in all directions at once. The action part of your plan comes with a mental attitude in your plan.

Your final question in your decision process may seem a bit anti-climactic:

(8) Am I ready to announce my decision?

Some people are able to answer this question readily. It is a clear proof of how *vigilantly* they have made their decision. They have searched for more than quick alternatives, they have filled out some balance sheets on pros and cons and weighed the difference carefully, they have done some soul searching for important preferences in their dilemma. And they are ready to go public.

I'm Doing My Best... But It Isn't Enough

For other people, this question is harder. Some indeed get "cold feet" at the last moment, reverse their stand or remain fixed. One young woman faced the dilemma of staying in a relationship with a man who controlled and abused her yet whom she somehow loved and could not leave. Over and over she came to the point of breaking things off, but just when she decided to tell him he would plead and cajole her, and she would reverse her decision and stay with him. This is a story told over and over again in marriages where there is alcoholism, wife-battering and other problems. People regrettably do not follow through with their own decisions. This is to say, *people often do not see this last question* (Am I ready to announce my decision?) *as part of the decision making process.*

In summary, these are the marks of a good decision: do it vigilantly. That is, have that amount of worry which will enable you to see the seriousness of risks in what you are deciding and to see all the options which you have. Entertain a moderated optimism, a conviction that a solution can be found which is somehow satisfying. And give yourself enough time to carry out your search of options and to reflect on your own deepest desires.

Then there are the steps or stages to follow as you ask all the questions of a vigilant search.

CHECK AGAIN WHAT *NOT* TO DO

There are styles of making a decision which you will want to avoid: panic, inertia and the forms of avoidance. Suppose you look again at these pitfalls, these self-defeating styles to make sure you know what *not* to do. Consider these styles in more detail.

Inertia becomes a self-defeating style when evidence is piling up that the danger is real: your marriage is getting painfully dissatisfying or your job is becoming intolerable. Inertia in the face of real facts of dire threats will hurt you in the long run. Don't give into the temptation to say, "No big Deal!" when the facts are clear and you could be a loser if things go on as they are. This is the point of the proverbial ostrich hiding his head in the sand.

Unworried change is a style of having insufficient precaution about jumping into a new path. Better known, it is a form of impulsiveness to avoid the work of worrying. This is seen in people who leave a job too quickly, without having another to go to; they are simply aware of the irritation they are leaving. Likewise some couples divorce because of very small incompatibilities ("she leaves her shoes all over the house") or family crises which can be rectified.

A very sage thought puts the matter well: "Half of life's problems come from saying 'yes' too soon and not saying 'no' soon enough." What is really at stake in this self-defeating style is not exploring enough routes or alternatives. A person does this because s/he wants to cut down alertness or cease the effort of a healthy search for new ways of his/her dilemma. The corrective for this style is keep the search going before you jump too soon.

Panic is for some people the style they are most likely to adopt when they get into a dilemma. Like the previous style this is a form impulsiveness. Panicking, however, is a veiled strength: the person who panics at least worries and is alert (painfully so).

Healthy alertness, nevertheless, is one thing and panic is another. Panic arises because of a "hyper" state of tension linked with the belief that there is not enough time. Panic leads to rapidly closing down your options, feeling mentally confused, and then trying to take in too much information at once.

Panic arises when you see there is a deadline closing in on you. The corrective for it is to give yourself as much time as you possibly can as a framework in which to look at your options — but *then to look at time!* Some people get themselves into a panicked state by first using the inert style, by delaying so long that the reality of what facts they were denying come crushing in on them; then they are forced to act.

Some stresses become distress because they come with a deadline imposed by others, for example, the deadline of handing in one's resignation or submitting a proposal, or for finalizing a divorce, for getting a loan, for helping a child turn his behavior around before he gets expelled from school, and so on. Time pressures permit a large proportion of people's distresses.

I'm Doing My Best... But It Isn't Enough 111

The main strategy, if you are prone to panic, is to make such none of the deadlines are imposed by *you*, and in an arbitrary fashion. Give them a healthy amount of time, while you keep yourself alert. Be careful not to add a deadline which is earlier than is necessary. One person had what she called her "three day theory." If a tough decision arose about one of her teen children, she would wait three days before taking any action. However upset she was about the dangers she saw her youths getting involved in, she would wait and "sleep on it" — not once but twice. She found she rarely rushed into a decision in a panicky way and found most of her decisions (which she worked through *with* them) something everyone could live with.

Avoidance. Here is a style that most decision makers can feel a kinship with. Everyone would like to avoid major decisions of a personal nature. As a result, people have devised so many ways to avoid decisions. But we can summarize some of these ways.

    *Showing lack of interest in the problems
     **Inattentive to signals of danger: avoid thinking about the problem
     **Distracting oneself by other activities such as by the "highs" of alcohol and other drugs, or by other activities ("busy work")
     **Procrastinating

    *Relying on others: buck passing

    *Ignoring information on the defects of what you have a "wish" to do and exaggerating attractive features about this option which actually is most questionable, called bolstering or rationalizing.

SUMMARY

In conclusion, avoid these styles: Panic on one extreme, Standing Pat, on the other; a Quick-shift (unworried change) or an Avoidance which either shows lack of interest, passes the buck, ignores the facts, or procrastinates too long. Now go over the steps in Decision Know-How.

Summary Of Steps In Decision Know-How

Start: HOW MAJOR DECISIONS GET STARTED: SOMETHING IS CHANGED!

STEP ONE: GET IT OUT!

* PRESERVES YOU FROM INERTIA, DOING NOTHING
* PRESERVES YOU FROM TOO RAPID A CHANGE
* KEEPS YOU CONCERNED, ALERT: VIGILANCE: WORRY!
* KEEPS YOU FLEXIBLE TO DIFFERENT OPTIONS: CLOSING DOWN TOO SOON

STEP TWO: GET A HANDLE BY ASKING QUESTIONS:

1) HOW MUCH TIME DO I HAVE?
   TIME DETERMINES IN LARGE PART WHICH STRATEGY YOU CHOOSE
2) WHAT ARE THE ALTERNATIVES AVAILABLE TO ME AS I SEE THEM NOW?
* STAY OR GO? I.E. TWO PART?
* IF YOU SEE MORE THAT IS A GOOD SIGN
* GO FROM THE NOW TO THE NEW: PRESERVES YOU FROM *PROCRASTINATION,* AVOIDANCE
* KEEPING IN CONTROL IS THE RESULT OF STARTING WITH THE RESULT OF STARTING WITH THE "NOW"
* PRESERVES YOU FROM *PANIC, SHIFTING, RESONSIBILITY*
3) WHAT ARE THE PROS AND THE CONS OF EACH ALTERNATIVE?
* THIS IS FAMILIAR GROUND: WE ALL DO THIS
* SPECIAL FEATURE OF "THE BALANCE SHEET" APPROVAL OF SELF
* THE SPECIAL TYPES OF PROS AND CONS

STEP THREE: BE RID OF RIGIDITY: GET A PERSPECTIVE

4) MAKE A STRATEGIC WITHDRAWAL, RELAX AND GET AWAY — FOR A TIME
5) NOW, WHAT IS IT I WANT TO BRING ABOUT WITH THIS DECISION?
* BALANCE SHEETS FORCE ME INTO SOME SOUL SEARCHING, PERSONAL AND PRACTICAL

*HOW A SINGLE ITEM OF ONE TYPE OF PRO CAN OUT-WEIGH A LARGE NUMBER OF NEGATIVES.
*WHAT FEW OUTCOMES DO I CHERISH THE MOST?
*WILL I COME OUT OF THIS DECISION BY PURELY RESTORING THE PAST, OR BETTER OFF? OR IN WORSE SHAPE.

STEP FOUR: STRENGTHEN YOURSELF

6) CAN I COME UP WITH ONE NEW, SUPERIOR?
*I'LL TALK TO TWO PEOPLE I KNOW; READ ONE ARTICLE DISCUSSING THE MATTER; VISIT ONE NEW RESOURCE.

STEP FIVE: MAKE A PLAN

7) IS ONE ALTERNATIVE NOW SUPERIOR?
8) ANY NEGATIVE RESULTS GOING TO DEVELOP IMMEDIATELY?
9) AM I READY TO DECLARE MY DECISION?
10) IMPORTANT PEOPLE: ARE THEY SUPPORTIVE, NOT IMPATIENT, OPTIMISTIC ACTIONS TO TAKE, ATTITUDES TO RE-SHAPE

Chapter Six

The Distressful Dilemmas of Feelings

In this chapter we will discuss very special kinds of stress and distress: those which arise from one's moods and feelings.

Emotional reactions are, to be sure, a part of all stress and every distress. Personal discomfort in one's feelings are so vivid that most people readily equate stress with emotional hurt and hassle. Nevertheless, some emotional turmoils are so significant as to constitute a stress or distress all unto themselves. Three forms of stress have been identified by Irving Janis (who contributed so much to the decision making of Chapter Five). He found that *fear, guilt* and *shame* are the most frequent sources of stress in everyday life.

STRESSES OF DAILY FEELINGS

The following people would agree with Janis that the above mentioned three feelings can indeed be forms of distress. They would add simply the feelings of hostility or anger to the list, but then, so does Janis.

> John is deeply worried about his upcoming divorce. He dreads the prospect of being alone, of loneliness. While convinced of the "rightness" of the decision and generally self confident in other areas, John experiences sheer fear on the single matter of loneliness.
>
> Sam is under the stress of his own feelings of hostility. He wakes up angry. His own feelings are a constant threat to his marriage.

I'm Doing My Best . . . But It Isn't Enough

Dianne is under the stress of her own moodiness: hostility but also resentment. She gets uncontrollably down. She feels she should be married; she is quite attractive but has not found a man she feels good toward: "the only ones I attract are losers."

Martha experiences a lot of stress of worry: more precisely she feels bad with shame feelings for flunking out of nursing school. Her family had counted so much on Martha to become a nurse. Her favorite aunt was a nurse. Martha herself never knew what she wanted, but now she has let her family down.

Helen feels shame too, not for anything she did but because her boyfriend flunked out of a military school — which greatly disappointed her parents. Helen feels the same shame vicariously.

Eddie is in the process of divorce and experiences the stress of a feeling, "I've been used, abused and neglected," by his wife no longer loving him.

Tanya feels the stress of guilt: her child was stillborn and perhaps the fact that she was on the pill too shortly before coming pregnant caused her fetus to spontaneously abort.

Bob feels the stress of guilt: he attempted suicide. Though it bothers him that others think poorly of him, what "bugs" him most, is that he violated what he himself thinks about taking his own life.

Fear, shame, guilt and anger are frequent forms emotional stress take. These are the feelings which daily cause us distress or at least moderate to severe discomfort. There are other emotions, to be sure. Indeed the two major forms of emotional stress are: anxiety and depression. Yet these two emotions have a strong mixture of the first group. I like to call fear, shame, guilt and anger "The Daily Feelings" and anxiety and depression "The Biggies." Whatever the emotion, however, we need a few words about understanding them as we start to cope with their stresses.

One thing about any kind of emotional stress is that it lays the totality of stress before you. Stress is first and last an emotional experience. Consider for example sheer fear, the first of the Daily Feelings. You may think of any fear you have: fear of people, failure, fatigue, rejection, crowds or whatever. That fear, like any emotion ties together everything about stress and what we have said. The same feeling will summarize also many of the coping strategies.

In a fear stress, first of all, threat predominates. We have the feeling because of some mental image of what might happen. The fear stress, secondly, discloses to you that your motives and needs are the real issue of stress and are here squarely at stake. Then again, fear and other feelings make us clearly aware that we are in conflict (Fact Two of our Map, in Chapter 4) and we are aroused or in a state of upsettedness (Fact Three).

Stress is all here, in emotional stress. Every step of our pesonal experience testifies that stress is an emotional experience. Our feelings, such as sheer fear, are testimony that we are in stress. Earlier in our portrait of stress we saw the parts of the picture, and they are tied together by feelings, such as fear or shame and the rest. Ailments are preceded by feeling; mental confusion is with feeling; behavior bears the mark of feeling.

If you are a Sam or Diane now and are churning with emotional upset, what I say on emotions may sound unhelpful. But if you are in a state of some inner quiet you will be able to become acquainted with some of your best friends, your emotions!

Emotions, our friends. One thing all emotions have in common is being misunderstood. Feelings have been given a bad reputation. Feelings are often spoken of as if they were active little things inside us which persist and cause troubles. In actual fact, our feelings can be an emormously helpful friend. Feelings can be a warning signal that we can use to see that something should be looked into. They can be the strong burst of energy we need. They can be the clue to what our conflicts are, where our expectations have misfired, and where now we should take some actions to change things. *We should live with these feelings for a time. To feel bad or fearful is not to cope poorly.*

I'm Doing My Best . . . But It Isn't Enough

When we look more closely to our real problems in emotional stresses, they turn out to be, not so much emotions, as some background causes of emotional states but the real problems in "emotional troubles" often surface as being: 1) expectations, sometimes unrealistic and sometimes unacknowledged, 2) unresolved conflicts, 3) memories of failure, 4) ineffective skills, 5) poorly defined attitudes, or 6) something we have learned which now needs to be reexamined. But our emotions will be a friendly reminder of what is wrong and what we can do.

FOUR FRIENDLY ATTITUDES TOWARDS FEELINGS

What really determines one's reaction to stress is our *pre*-stress personality. We should come to emotional stresses with at least four healthy attitudes toward our feelings.

1. Begin to trust your feelings. They supply the tools of motivation you need to change and improve your condition. They are helpful signals. The following are some reasons why we should trust our feelings in stress.

   *The mark of successful copers is that they have their feelings accessible to them.

   *Successful copers are in touch with a wide variety of feelings.

   *Successful copers' decision making is actually better than unemotional copers.

   *Successful copers put their feelings into words; they, therefore, experience fewer ailments.

   *Successful copers count on the energy of their feelings, at least to get them started.

2. Emotions expressed improve our perceptions. Emotions are almost always triggered by our perceptions, our evaluations of what is happening to us. Feelings are the result of ideas. Our attitudes may be distorted, rarely do our emotions become so. Attitudes need to be corrected, checked, re-fashioned; much less do our emotions need to be rectified. The implications of *using* our feelings are these:

   *Successful copers put their feelings into words.

*Successful copers "work through" their feelings: airing them, they have the chance to correct their perceptions. Feelings are admitted, acknowledged, faced, and paired with the situations and thoughts which come with the feelings.

3. Feelings are a wide variety. Some feelings are spoken of so often that they are seen as the only ones. For example, when I say "He's emotional," what comes to your mind? Possibly you will think first of sadness or elation — a tribute to your basic bent toward pessimism or optimism. But anxiety and anger are surely first to come to most people — a fact which makes them and all emotions doubly misunderstood. Consider how much a part of your treasured life are the following feelings:

*Enthusiasm   *Trust
*Excitement   *Relief
*Surprise   *Relaxation
*Joy   *Curiosity
*Fascination

4. Stress of emotions comes from its duration. We know we are in stress when we are troubled. It is a state of emotional unpleasantness. The stress comes from the duration, with which comes intensity. Anxiety, for example, may heretofore have been unnoticeable, inconspicuous or at least tolerable — not to say "friendly." Now it seems vivid and intolerable.

Any emotional state, fed on long standing notions, can arrive at an intolerable pitch. If it does so, the emotional pain can be experienced. The emotional pain has the effects of being disorganizing, crippling, even destructive. The emotion lasts too long, returns too frequently, or is evoked by too many incidents. *But the problem comes because we have not acted on the emotions, have not trusted them and used them.*

Prolonged emotional tension can do damage, such as leaving us depressed, hopeless, pessimistic; other tangible damage is in our ailments of headaches, the tissue damage of ulcers, hypertension or even psychosomatic illnesses.

Prolonged emotional tension can have another effect; *fatigue* or exhaustion. There are different kinds of fatigue, as we indicated elsewhere: physical, mental and subjective.

Overview of coping with emotional stresses. If you discover that your stresses are of the emotional kind, you are in a position to use every strategy we have used so far. I would summarize your "attack" on your stresses as two-pronged. *First, there are actions to take; second, there are attitudes to shape.*

Actions to take include the five step approach discussed earlier when dealing with a crisis, in Chapter Three. This means, in summary, "Getting It Out," finding someone to talk to; "Getting a Handle," which in an emotional stress is invariably finding either a conflict or frustration; then there is the need to "Get The Knots Untied," particularly because in your emotional state you need to rid yourself of rigidity; you also need to "Regain Your Strengths," and know that the strength in emotions is having them accessible (often gained by getting them out, to a friend); finally, you will have to make a decision.

In emotional stresses, there are also attitudes to shape. This means knowing your three vulnerabilities of your needs, your resources and your working beliefs. You will need to keep active the attitudes of the "Big Three:" the attitude of seeking new information, retaining autonomy, and regaining your balance. It is this approach of shaping attitudes will ensure you of a lifestyle for dealing with stresses, and coming out of emotional stresses better and stronger.

Let us begin with John's stress of sheer fear, mentioned a few pages back. John and you, if you suspect yours is a fear stress, can take the following steps. All you need to do is to identify first what it is you fear, as John did.

STRESS OF SHEER FEAR

John was worrying greatly about being alone. He married early at the age of 19. He had not dated seriously many girls before courting Helen who was to become his wife. Now, at age 44, conflicts which had been present all along have become unbearable. He and Helen have grown miles apart with no hope of reconciliation. John is fully satisfied that divorce is an appropriate decision, but he is frightened at the thought of being socially active alone, and is simply terrified at the prospect of attempting to find another companion.

John's stress is the threat of a "sheer fear." He is very distressed about this worry, which is actually quite realistic. There is good news for John, as there is for anyone suffering under a fear or phobia. The good news is that some very helpful techniques are available to help a person with a fear. The help comes from the one thing recognized about fear stress: that is, the fear is about something *specific*, very particular. For John, his fear is about socializing, meeting people and keeping relationships going.

The main advantage in a fear stress is that we can identify that which we fear. As long as we can do that, we can set up a specific set of strategies for dealing with sheer fear. I must add that these strategies may indeed become clear, though this is not to say they are easy. They may be hard, and sometimes a fear gets so crippling that a person needs professional help. Nevertheless, there is definite help for a person with a strong fear — even though this is not always "self help" in all cases.

The following are some steps which John — and you, if you suspect you have a fear stress — can take. All you need do is identify first what it is that you fear.

Steps for Sheer Fear Stress. Once a person has identified what his or her fear is about, s/he can take the following steps which are based on the model given earlier in Chapter Three.

> 1. Get it out. John should talk about his fears. Expectations will be revealed to himself. He will face this expectation of being absolutely miserable when all alone, that he will be totally unable to meet new friends or to tolerate loneliness. Memories of failure and ineffective skills may be faced. This is not a solution but it is a start to one. For he will also probably gain awareness (by talking about it) that his fear is exaggerated, that he will not be totally inept nor completely miserable alone, that he *does* have strengths which will become clear at the later steps.
>
> 2. Get a handle. John feels that he, like most people with a sheer fear, is frustrated. That is, he is up against a barrier

that he cannot get around. In this case, he experiences a barrier which is a *lack* within himself. (Frustration #4 of Chapter Four) He needs to start basic decision making steps, which first means exploring some options. For example, one option is to look for the familiar people he still will have in his life; also, to look into what he really knows he enjoys doing alone.

3. Get less uptight. For many persons with a strong fear, this is the most important step. With fear, confusion and the natural reaction of becoming rigid (mentally and emotionally) sets in. John needs to apply specific relaxation skills, to get a better handle on the stress and to develop further ways of coping with the threat he faces and fears.

a) John should do muscle relaxation exercises, such as the one found earlier in Chapter Two, Figure 2-2. Once or twice is not sufficient; they must be repeated, at first daily.

b) Use the "So What If" technique. John notices himself saying, *"What if* I am alone? *What if* I can find no one to talk to? *What if* I'm socially clumsy?" If he adds, "So" he has the helpful phrase, *"So what if* I'm alone?" Well, he may feel bad but it is not the end of the world. He can watch television, visit friends, take a trip, go to movies. There are lots of things which do not require a partner.

4. Shore up resources. John should examine his resources and pull them together. In Chapter Seven we say these to be in self, other people, and the community at large.

a) resources in himself are gained by recalling positive stimulations he has dealt with socially; new friends he has made; compliments he has received from others; initiative he has taken with others;

b) people resources. John should see his friends as forming three concentric circles, as indicated in Chapter Seven. On the outer circle are those who are casual acquaintances; the second inner circle are those he has spent some personal, chosen time with; in the inner circle are close friends he can share with and can depend on. He should try to contact people in the second and third area, asking for their support and understanding.

c) community. John can look into his community or neighborhood for resources. Social groups such as Parents Without Partners, Un-Married Adults. Better still, he can look for training opportunities at local centers or colleges for overcoming shyness, developing social skills.

5) Make an action plan. John might start to decide what he is going to *do,* to prepare for his time when he is alone.

a) He uses the set of decisions offered at the end of Chapter Three, deciding what things he is going to drop, start, plan, resume, dare.

b) He decides to buy the book by Philip Zimbardo, *Shyness.*

c) He decides to take an assertiveness training course, and calls the local mental health association — his resource.

SHAME AND GUILT

Your stress is one of shame when you face the threat of other people criticising you for reasons such as not suiting them, living up to their standards or not being included by them. This is the kind of stress which means a threat to your *needs* for being invited, welcomed, included, and esteemed by others.

On the other hand, your stress is one of guilt when you see a threat that you are not living up to your *own* standards. You suffer the pain of self-accusations. You begin to lose respect in your own eyes. There is a big gap between the ideals you have chosen for yourself and the kind of person you find yourself to be.

Shame and guilt appear so similar. They even seem to have the same connections in our nervous system. Yet they are important to separate, for each is highly involved in its own kind of stress. And when we later come to the two "biggies" of emotional stress, anxiety and depression, we will find them playing a big part in these.

I'm Doing My Best . . . But It Isn't Enough

Martha, mentioned at the start of this chapter, shows how clearly a person can get into a shame stress. In fact, some people tend to get into an entire life style where they live to please others, and thereby get locked into a life of shame stress. Among all the steps they will need to take, none is more important than an "Attitude Shape-up."

SHAME STRESS

In my helping role as a therapist I find many persons who are in the stress where they say, "I feel used, put upon, scorned, treated with contempt." It is often at the end of a love relationship, sometimes it is men but more often women. The stress of being rejected is the stress of shame.

There is also the stress of shame as found in the teenage boy who bites his fingernails and suffers the shame of holding a report before his classmates or holding hands with a girl. It is real stress to him.

Stress in a real sense is in the eye of the beholder because of our own personal needs and outlooks. But shame particularly makes stress in the eye of the beholder: it is a threat which comes from the eyes of *other* beholders!

The stress of shame is the emotional hurt of seeing some "other" as the source of contempt, scorn or ridicule. Some person, for whom we feel something emotionally, appears as a powerful and ridiculing being. That person is seen as superior and proud while we feel weak and small.

And so in this stress we may "get small," or so it seems that way. We may turn our head to the side and downward, eyes turned ascant and eyelids lowered or perhaps held partly closed from time to time. If it is a slight and light ridicule we may blush, but if it is severe scorn, so as to be stress, we experience pure inadequacy and confusion. From this may come depression or, equally, soothing hostility or revenge.

Shame in its purest form is a sensitive *self-consciousness* that we did not suit somebody else. This is the key to remember, for we can use this self-consciousness or be lost in it. The awareness of not living up to someone else is the clue to how to cope in the stress of being rejected by a lover, over-looked for a promotion, not included socially, or being ridiculed.

A shame stress is the time to ask two questions. First, do I really want and need to suit *that* person(s)? Second, what do *I* feel about that which is the object of disfavor?

Here are some things that run through people's minds when they feel shame, as found by Izard, an expert on emotions. Are any on your mind?

- a failure or disappointment
- having done something to hurt others
- something wrong or stupid
- having some unclean, immoral though
- doing something legally or morally wrong, harmful
- doing nothing when others think something should be done

Steps in Shame Stress. If it appears that you are in a Shame Stress, you will be in a situation similar to Martha's: she flunked out of school. You feel you have failed in the eyes of others. You have not lived up to other's expectations.

A. ACTIONS TO TAKE

1. Get it out. Talk about your feelings about letting others down to someone who simply listens and passes no judgment. In these stresses perhaps more than any other, there is the need for being with a person who lets *you* come up with your own understanding of the problem and your own solutions. You will begin to see there is a lot of useless shame and that it is not possible to please everyone. But at the outset, live for a short while with your feeling of shame. It has this strength: It guarantees you are socially sensitive and people are important to you, though perhaps too many.

2. Get a handle. You are probably experiencing the stress of Frustration #1, discussed in Chapter Four. Martha's stress is like that: there is a barrier from within oneself. For Martha and many with the stress of shame, the threat is from a personal limitation. Sometimes this limitaton comes from having goals, not of one's own, but knowing this is the stress leads a person to the first step in a solution: changing one's goals. After she admitted she wanted to become a nurse because her parents or

I'm Doing My Best . . . But It Isn't Enough 125

favorite aunt wanted her, she is in a position to start seeking what she wanted. The failure, or barrier, was to live up to other's expectations.

Here is the unique problem of shame stress: our attitude. This is the clue to seeing that the major coping strategy will be to examine one's attitude toward ciriticism of others. So a person with a shame stress should particularly attend to the Long Term Strategy, Attitudes you can shape, and clear up the attitude about Fear of Criticism.

3. Get less uptight. This will be the same as with a fear: do a relaxation exercise. Also valuable is the "So What If" technique, discussed on Fear Stresses.

B. ATTITUDES TO SHAPE — IN SHAME STRESS

The kind of threat presented by shame stresses particularly involves our attitudes, which need to be re-shaped. It means asking some hard questions and giving some clear answers to how much we expect from other people, how much we depend on them to meet our needs, whether they can, after all, meet our needs, whether we want to please them as we are now.

Martha's stress arose because she carried in herself a self defeating attitude: that she was to please, at all costs, her family. She cultivated the feeling that her own worthwhileness comes from outside herself, from other people. Their praise makes her good, their blame makes her "bad." Or so it seems to her. She needs to sort out her attitudes about what others can or should be to her.

The shameful Marthas of life need perhaps most of all to know the saying, "He (or she) who trims himself to suit everyone will soon whittle himself away." One of the first things to do in attitude shaping about stress of shame is to *examine the consequences* of trying to please someone we really might not wish to please.

Reflections on a shame-induced attitude. We have spoken of fears before. But here we have another. There is one special, particular fear which is so far reaching and rangy that I can only call it our Wide-Angle Fear, much like a camera lens of this name which scans an entire room, a total mountain or building. Understanding this single fear is enough to make us believe that G.B. Shaw was right, "It is easy — terribly easy — to shake a man's faith in himself." This fear can and does shake millions of people's faith in themselves; we can grasp it in, of all places, clothes fashions.

Fashion is one way to shake a person's self-confidence. We each have our own level of the need to be fashionable. We may chuckle about it, thinking with Oscar Wilde, "Fashion is a form of ugliness so intolerable that we have to alter it every six months." But for others, an absolute terror awaits them if they are found unfashionable in clothes. Behind the fear of being unfashionable is our Wide Angle Fear: *the fear of being criticized and shamed.*

I may decide to buy a suit, for example not because my present clothes are worn out, not even because I am enamored of the new style. I buy it because of what people will say. It is not even so much what people will say, if we buy the suit, that spurs us into fashions. What prods us is the fear of what they will say if we are not fashionable. This is our quivering fear to be criticized, and that clothes fashions can have deep effects in a person indicates just how easy it is to "shake a man's (or woman's) faith in himself."

Shame stresses will particularly abound when being fashionable is important, where flaunting an image is held to be of high value. At such a time there will be a rapid tendency to develop a wide-angle fear of criticism and dread of shame. Shame is directly related to how indiscriminate a person is in trying to please others. Such persons develop the wide-angle fear of dreading to be shamed by everyone.

A wide-angle fear of shame harms us in two ways for coping. First, this vague and indiscriminate fear makes us do anything to avoid blame from anyone. A person will be careful to do nothing which annoys, will take no stand which antagonizes. The real harm herein is that one loses touch with their own real wants, talents and strengths. So, the action of "shoring up strengths" becomes particularly difficult for a person with a wide angle fear of criticism.

Secondly, a wide angle fear of criticisms takes away a person's persistence. The Marthas of life may be good starters but they are poor finishers. They become "losers." They lost capacity for *motivation* — which mostly means the

I'm Doing My Best . . . But It Isn't Enough

capacity to stay with something over a long period. A lack of persistence often means a spirit has been broken. A random wide angle fear of criticism, of "public opinion" shakes a person's confidence in themselves, thereby diminishing persistence.

And because persistence is central to a person's developing his or her identity, a large fear of shame and criticism tends to erode any feelings of identity. A person literally tends to live through others.

We all fear being criticized. The level of this fear indicates our threat to being vulnerable to the stress of criticism. For most people this fear is fairly strong. We may indeed admit to our little faults but that is to persuade people we have no large ones. The fear I speak of spreads like cancer; if fear for our clothes is tender, what will fear of criticism of our competence, our skills, our reliability bring?

The fear is normal enough. Not all fears are to be feared. We can normally fear all sorts of things, particularly when people are involved. Driving too fast, not meeting our bills, insulting our mate: these bring criticism (at least!) from the patrolman, car dealer and spouse. Being a "social animal" means just this: no one is immune to the influence of people. Most animals are social; what makes humans unique socially is the susceptibility to influence, i.e. approval and criticism, from others. If the "susceptibility" is high it becomes a threat and can become a stress.

Wherever there can be a mistake, an incompetent step or a failure to meet the expectations of others, there can be criticism and therefore a fear of it. A person who can fall can fear it. If we can fear the fall, we can fear being criticized for the fall. And then this normal fear can work for our health or our ruin

The shame fear can be either a flower or a weed. Weed shame is random, found everywhere, coming from everyone. Like a wide indiscriminate shame can spread indefinitely. Psychologist Albert Ellis has identified a large number of attitudes which really makes for irrational fears and shames.

The shame fear can be a flower of a healthy shame fearing a selected group of people's comments and criticisms. Their criticism is selective and has the effect of pruning.

The strength of a healthy fear of criticism can induce some pause in what we do, some healthy hesitation in taking steps which we are at first inclined to. Others disagree with our plans: perhaps they know something we do not know? Perhaps we have not gathered all the facts.

Healthy shame is one of the feelings which will help us become better decision makers. Healthy, discriminate shame enables us to do some of the "beforehand worry" which is necessary for all good decision makers.

Mature stress coping is not achieved through fear, though a dash of it may help. A healthy fear of selective shame tells us what we want to avoid, what we are turning FROM. A healthy fear is simply our awareness of something we value and can destroy in ourselves. The healthy fear then leads us to good coping: learning to handle fears is to learn to handle what we value. We can control our fears.

THE GUILT STRESS

And then there is guilt. It is a feeling so similar to shame yet so different, as we have said. But guilt is special because when it is a stress, shame may confuse our thoughts temporarily, whereas guilt can hang on. Guilt seems to stimulate thought, even brooding. Guilt can become a preoccupation which paralyzes.

Recall Tanya's stress over the loss of her child, which she attributed to her staying on the pill too long. Her guilt was the heavy threat which came because she felt responsible. In addition, Tanya experienced guilt because she had set certain standards by which she wanted to live, for the well-being of both her baby and herself.

Tanya's stress surfaces the two major features of a guilt stress: responsibility and standards. Whereas shame is felt because of what other people say and feel (or what we *expect* of them), guilt comes from what we see in ourselves. We are really feeling we have failed to live up to our own standards, and we could have.

Looked at more closely, persons feel guilt in one of two ways: either they feel they failed because they did something they should not have (example: taking the pill too near to conception), or they did not do something they should have (taken proper exercise).

Which Stresses Are Those Of Guilt?

*Many guilt stresses are experienced after decisions of an important nature, such as attending to someone we care about (both Tanya's and Bob's stresses); or divorcing, leaving a job, doing something dishonest.

*If a person is depressed, there is probably a heavy dosage of guilt. The person feels worthless and a failure. Likewise, if a person ruminates excessively about the past, guilt is often involved.

*If a person experiences long-standing confusion, worry and helplessness, guilt may also be a central ingredient here.

*If a person experiences *Burn-our* or *Overload* stresses (discussed in the eighth chapter), guilt for not working hard enough to meet standards set by themselves is very likely involved.

*If a person experiences stress because of inadequate skills or training (for example with people or computers) they may be experiencing guilt.

*If a person has violated some rule or moral code (having an affair, not fulfilling a religious requirement) guilt is clearly involved.

Coping with guilt requires more than this book can adequately cover. If your guilt is severe, you may need to seek professional help or work over some matters with someone knowledgeable with one of the two pivots of guilt, your own standards. Standards which bring guilt into play are usually of a moral and/or religious nature. You may need to talk with your minister, priest or rabbi, to fully understand your own standards.

I cannot here provide you with a set of standards, nor should I. What I can do is suggest some ways in which you can cope with your feelings of guilt which are centered around those standards. That is, once you know what your standards or values are, I can provide some suggestions on how to live by them — and not be paralyzed by them; how to cope with life's threats to those standards — and to come out of such threats better and stronger; how to *adapt* your values to your needs for living.

Let me just add about knowing your own standards and values: one of the most important tools of self-help is found in value-clarification.

Guilt May Be Useless Or A Strength

There is a lot of needless guilt, self-imposed without reason. Guilt is "without reason" when it is felt because of unrealistic expectation or because of unrealistic responsibility. So, guilt today has a bad reputation. "Guilt trips" are wasted trips of pain. And some popular writers go so far as to call guilt a totally "useless" emotion. Until recently one of the few references that psychologists made to religion was to refer to its unwarranted guilt messages. The guilt arising from religion of the past has indeed probably been excessive. And yet — there may be another side to guilt. Rather, there may be another form of guilt.

I would suggest that even your guilt has its strengths. If you feel guilt this means that you have some standards, and you feel bad about not living up to those standards. Such a feeling is not, I submit, useless. No one can really live without personal standards. There is good reason to think that neither you nor I can be mentally healthy without standards — and therefore have the possibility, the susceptibility of guilt when we do not choose by those standards. (There is a name for people who try to live without standards and guilt: sociopaths. They cause a lot of stress to others). But more than anything else guilt has the strength of being the basis of your responsibility to people.

So we need to be very clear about guilt, neither to dismiss it nor to exaggerate it. It is real, freighted with stress but also the bearer of an enormous *good* feeling about yourself. For example, if I know you can and do experience guilt, I know three things about you: that you have accepted some ethical values, that you cultivate a sense of responsibility to abide by these values, and you have a sufficient ability to see differences between what you want to do and actually do. I would choose you for a friend. These are strengths, my friend.

Tanya's guilt was focused on the past. Bob's guilt has another focus, the present and near future. His guilt makes him anticipate, look forward to care for his father.

I'm Doing My Best . . . But It Isn't Enough

Most of the needless or, if you choose, "useless" guilt is of Tanya's kind. It is a stress which is self-defeating because the Tanyas of life cannot really undo the past, though they can learn from it.

So, guilt is a very complicated matter. Volumes have been written of it and for the interested reader I would suggest Izard's *Human Emotions* (1977) as a splendid review of this and most emotions.

But briefly, guilt has good news and bad news. The bad news is that "it is (only) severe and chronic guilt or an extremely low guilt threshold that leads to serious psychological problems and maladjustment" (Izard). Guilt also gets so intertwined with other feelings such as anxiety, hostility, aggression and other negative feelings as to seem inseparable. The good news, however, is that to experience some kind of guilt is to display a higher level of personal growth potential. It also means we can take another person's point of view.

In spite of what you hear, do not dispense with a healthy dose of guilt. No, it does not feel good. But it does enable you to come out of life's problems better, stronger.

Steps in Guilt Stress. If it appears yours is a guilt stress, you will be seeing yourself in a situation similar to either Tanya's or Bob's. You will be worrying about a failure either in the past or a possible failure upcoming. Your two major coping techniques will be found in the action of "getting a handle" and in attitude re-shaping.

1) ACTIONS TO TAKE

1. Getting guilt out by talking about it is probably one of the hardest things to do. Still, speaking about the guilt feeling may also be one of the most valuable. If you are at all a person of good judgment (and I assume you are), you will know that "Love means never having to say you're sorry" is a total error. It is valuable to say we are sorry. In addition to all the other benefits of expressing any feeling, saying we feel guilty strangely has another effect: that of unburdening us and a cleansing, if you please. Often, expressing our guilt when a friendship or love has been affected also is a step toward rebuilding that relationship — sometimes, not always.

2. Getting a handle on the guilt feeling. This is a most important step in coping with guilt. *What is it that you feel guilty about?* Are you a Tanya or a George: feeling a failure over something past or something upcoming. In a sense explained earlier, your handle is probably seeing your guilt as a Frustration (#1): something is seen as lacking within you.

3. Getting less uptight may be useful but is less likely to help in guilt stress than in fear stress.

4. Shoring up your strengths is definitely important. You need most to know your worthwhileness. You need to live consciously with the image that, though you may have failed, you are still a worthy, good, capable person. One of the most helpful experiences is that of Dov Elkins.

5. Make an action plan. If yours is a guilt stress, you probably should not make an action plan until after you have cleared up what your values and standards are and have worked through the following section of re-shaping your attitudes. You might also want to discuss your feelings first with a professional, in mental health and/or religious area.

"Half the troubles in life," quipped Josh Billings, "can be traced to saying 'Yes' too quickly or not saying 'No' soon enough." Most of us know what he meant out of our own raw experiences. Either a Yes or No comes back to haunt us in *consequences*. Our guilt points to those consequences. We need help to clear up our attitudes on the consequences, and therefore the guilt.

2) ATTITUDES TO SHAPE

Guilt is felt when you feel *responsible* for some misdoing. There are three helpful questions you can ask yourself to determine the guilt and put it in a healthy perspective:

*Was it foreseeable?
*Was it avoidable?
*Was there an obligation to avoid it?

For example, remember a homey instance when you left the rake out in the yard and a neighbor hurt himself on it? You may have been troubled by the guilt of it all. Well, was this accident foreseeable? Possibly but maybe not. If you know that he comes across your yard nightly (with your approval), then the accident was foreseeable. If it was so rare a walk for him, then it was not foreseeable; thus no responsibility, so dislodge yourself of any guilt.

But suppose you know it was foreseeable, the next question is: was it avoidable? Perhaps not. You may have left it there through no fault of your own, called away by an emergency and did not have time to think about putting away the rake. No responsibility, and thus no guilt is called for.

Now suppose you could have avoided it. Did you have an obligation to avoid leaving the rake there? To put the answer facetiously, there is probably neither a personal ethic or religious code about leaving rakes in the yard. So, no obligation sums up for no reason for guilt. (Legally, it may be quite a different matter! But guilt, for present purposes, is not to be governed by civic laws.)

These are three questions which begin to help a person see if his guilt is appropriate.

However, these three questions have a serious limitation, as stated. They really belong as guidelines *before* we act. A person should not consider healthy appraisal as a matter of hindsight. Acting responsibly means we conduct ourselves in terms of what we presently know, for *future* conduct. A twenty year old adult, on learning for the first time that something he did at the age of twelve hurt someone does not then become guilty.

We all need to rid ourselves of needless guilt, and this means particularly the misdoings of the past.

Stress of Guilty Parents

There are so many things which happen that good-minded people feel guilty about and should not — in matters for which they are not responsible. Consider parents, if you will. So many little hurts and bruises that come to the children simply cannot be avoided, because they cannot be foreseen. There is no possibly way to plot, at the start of a day, the paths and impulses of a six year old. Parents cannot watch the child all the time.

In fact, parents will harm the child emotionally and mentally by over-protectiveness. Parents try their best to put injurious medicines out of the way, to forbid crossing the street, and so forth. But when they have done that, which seems so little to help avoid injury, there remains more (much more) that is not foreseeable, and certainly not avoidable.

Decisions For Guilt Stress & Dilemmas

Is Tanya's guilt appropriate? Let's examine this. Was it foreseeable at the time that being on the pill shortly before attempting a pregnancy might result in her fetus being stillborn? Since this finding was not available to her in the sixties, she could not foresee this possibility. She can ask herself, "How was I to know?" Likewise, Was it avoidable? is another question. Due to financial circumstances, she wanted to avoid pregnancy until the time she decided to attempt it. All in all, she had no control, no responsibility and therefore no guilt.

Tanya can indeed conclude to no reasons for guilt. Still, saying it will not perhaps make it so, that is, diminish her guilt. At least saying it *once* will not take away the guilt. But repeating the reassurance will gradually help her to feel less guilty. Sometimes it does; sometimes the solution to such guilt does consist in an insight, a moment of understanding which is in fact a reassurance.

For Bob, the same three questions can be of use: Was it foreseeable that his father would be taken ill immediately after Bob's return home? Obviously not. Was it avoidable (even if foreseeable) that Bob would have to absent himself from his father? Not in this case. Likewise Bob can make a decision, not to feel guilty about being absent from his father. he will have to repeat the decision over and over, in order for it to be a solution (or a softening) to his guilt. It all comes down to his Control and Responsibility.

You will have to decide for yourself, in your particular set of circumstances, the answers to the three questions. Was your failure foreseeable, avoidable and was there an obligation to do other than you did?

DEPRESSION STRESS

This is the "Biggie" stress, the stress with which we are all familiar. If you suspect that your stress is depression, and it is severe, I would at this point like to suggest at the outset that you consider talking to a mental health professional. I cannot, in this modest book, help with your severe depression. I can at most help you understand some of the things which go into it, but you could no longer trust me if I were to be glib about your depression. Trust no one who says they can rid you of depression with a few pages of reading.

On the other hand, if your depression is moderate, "join the club," as they say. We all experience depression. The only people who claim not to are those who run away in frenetic activity. They are depressed all right, they just claim not to be.

By this time, we can get briefly to the point of what the coping with depression will be: First, getting a handle on it, getting it out; Secondly, shaping up our attitudes and mental images; Thirdly, taking some action. Suppose we look at depressed Daniel.

> Dan came in saying his main problem seemed to be that he did not have much energy any more. He felt himself to be a failure at his work; there were problems because he was in a small private real estate business which was owned by another man and his father — Leon and Harry. Daniel got along well with Leon but both had difficulty with the intrusions of Leon's father, Harry. Dan was thinking of leaving and getting a job elsewhere.
>
> More than at work, Dan felt he was not a good father to his two children; he also felt unattentive to his wife. He seemed to have lost a "caring attitude." Further, he didn't seem to have any interests anymore. He was depressed.

When we began to separate the parts of Dan's depression, we came up with these statements:

— He tends to bottle up his feelings
— He takes pains to hurt others' feelings even when he feels he has been injured

— People take advantage of him
— If someone were annoying him, he would smother his feelings rather than express his own feelings
— If in a disagreement, he is greatly afraid of his own reactions, fearing he will shake all over

You will notice that Daniel lacks confidence and perhaps skills in social situations. When Dan calls himself depressed two things particularly seem to be bothering him: his feelings which he holds in and his timidity in situations with other people. His further lack of interests seems to be the *result* of his locked feelings and social ineptitude.

The Depression Mix. We must begin by having some understanding of what depression is. Depression is actually many things, lumped together. This is what makes depression so difficult to cope with, let alone cure. Depression is a mix of thoughts, feelings and behaviors. If we were to sum it all up, depression might be seen in this little formula: D=P+S

Depression   equals   Pessimism   plus   Sadness

Pessimism

The first thing we should know about depression is that it seems to start "in our head." Some of the major contributions of depression are a state of mind. A person develops negative attitudes towards him or herself. Such a person also begins to cultivate negative attitudes toward the past and the future. Indeed, their major preoccupaton is, not with the present, but the past or future. The attitude is one of pessimism.

"Things will never get better" becomes the by-line. It is usually blended with feelings and thoughts we have already discussed: shame and guilt.

Sadness

Sadness is probably the biggest problem in life. After all, it is the absence of pleasure. Sadness is brought on by anything difficult, by any failure but especially by any loss. The difficulty of maintaining a family life, of getting a diploma or degree, of keeping an income, of handling a marital conflict or raising a child — any of these and much more can bring on sadness, and therefore depression.

I'm Doing My Best... But It Isn't Enough

Sadness in some ways represents to a person a basic failure or loss in life itself. Sadness is for some reason the very opposite of living. And when we look at the highest moments of living, they usually involve other people: family, loved ones, people whom we share respect and admiration with.

The biggest cause of sadness is probably loneliness. Just as people are the biggest source of pleasures for most people, the absence of people in one's life is the biggest source of sadness and, accordingly, depression.

We cannot live long in sadness. We will try to overcome it if we can, by some form of happiness wherein we recapture what was lost. We can also try to run from it — flee through sleep, avoidances, and other escapisms like alcohol and other drugs, and other intoxicating activities which keep us active and sometimes mindless.

Some amount of depression must be sustained. We must live with it, tolerate it, and "bear it."

Sustaining depression, however, always needs one necessary antidote: *hope*. If a person has difficulty sustaining themselves in depression it is a suggestion that they have slight hope. The entire groundwork of depression seems to rest on hope — or the lack thereof. And in many ways the solution to depression involves reviving hope.

Hope is the high probability of attaining an important goal. The amount of hope a person has depends upon two things (1) that the goal is important, and (2) there is a high likelihood of gaining it. If the goal is not important, there will be no hope, just indifference.

But if the goal is important, yet with little chance to be attained, then we experience anxiety, and this can be a part of depression too. Depression often has a high degree of restlessness with it. Anxiety means that the goal is still important but the likelihood of success is going down.

We can raise hope in two ways: (1) by making the goal more important, and (2) by increasing the chances for gaining what we want.

In brief, to be saddened is to be in a *weakened* condition. It is to be with lessened hope.

Solution to depression. The bulk of solutions for depression comes in the form of some kind of strength-finding. Solutions to depression will come by way of feelings and actions. The feeling most helpful is *anger* directed in constructive channels, by actions which consist in doing something, taking initiative, regaining control. There is, then, a limit to how much help in depression comes from purely talking about one's miseries, losses or failures.

One of the major forms of solutions to depression comes in *assertiveness skills*. Because a person who is depressed is one who is weakened and has a little hope, there is often an overdose of shyness or timidity. The depressed person needs to assert him or herself (Chapter Nine).

Another solution to depression comes in "shaping up" attitudes, which gives rise to the person's feelings of sadness. The depressed person is filled with learned ideas and images: negative images of themselves, low self esteem; negative in the sense of blaming themselves with excessive guilt and shame; negative in gloomy forecasts of future outcome and dismal memories of the past; negative in picturing personal helplessness, or lack of control.

So these solutions take the form of unlearning *learned helplessness*. For these solutions, professional therapy is usually in order. A person can rarely change these patterns of thoughts and images on one's own. Reading surely won't do it. One needs not insight, but an experience which will change our thoughts and images about several subjects: ourselves, our past, our future, our attitudes and beliefs, and so on.

Steps for depression. In brief the solutions for your depression will center around three steps: first, getting a handle on what your own sadness and depression are and where they come from; secondly, shaping up your attitudes and mental images; and thirdly, taking some action, making some plans and doing something.

A) ACTIONS TO TAKE

1. Get it out. Certainly this is very important, just as we have indicated it is important for any emotion. Two special features of getting depression out are these. On the one hand, talking about our depression is particularly important for us to surface our pessimistic thoughts and

I'm Doing My Best ... But It Isn't Enough

for "getting a handle" on what particular thoughts we are having. On the other hand, we should know there is a limit to how much help talking about our miseries will be: talking about one's depression reaches the point of diminishing returns. Once you have satisfied yourself that you have 'told your story' to your listening friend and he or she understands, then get ready to act. Some people get stuck here and want to go over their blues again and again, which ceases to help them at that point but indeed makes them more and more unhappy. You will have a good listening friend if he or she brings an end to commiserating at some point and says, "I think I understand now. Let's make a plan to do something."

2. Get a handle. Is your pessimism related to your thoughts about yourself? About your future? Your past? This is a most important coping step with depression.

3. Get less uptight. As with shame and guilt, this step may be less needed than with fear, unless you feel particularly tense.

4. Shore up your strengths. This is the end product of most coping strategies. To achieve this, move on to Attitude Shape Up.

B) ATTITUDES TO SHAPE

*The biggest cause of depression seems to be loneliness. Look into your personal resources: the people in your life. Identify anyone you can count on. Then, take the initiative and call them. Don't wait for the telephone to ring. Let them know you would like to be with them.

*Just as people are the biggest source of pleasure for most people, so their absence is the biggest source of sadness. Make a list of the best memories you have had which include people. Recall those memories in detail, the dates and times and situations.

*Make a set of decisions around people of your past that you can contact again, such as the decisions mentioned in Chapter Two.
— "Maybe I don't need to wait for them to contact me anymore."

— "Maybe I need to invite them out or to my place soon."
— "Maybe I do need to retain time with them _____." (movie going, luncheon, etc.)
— "Maybe I need to resume _____." (miniature golf, dancing)
— "Maybe I need to dare _____." (sending them a card to let them know I'm thinking of them)

*Important as people are, realize the limits to which others can be to your loneliness. A person can indeed be lonely in a crowd. Part of your "loneliness" may actually be aloneness, the basic part of any separate human being. Relish that and learn to enjoy being by yourself. Restrict your self-pity about being alone. Everyone is alone at times. It is probably only when we can use being alone constructively that we are really able to bring something to others when we are together.

*Just as some aloneness is our lot, so is some depression. Be patient with it, do not try escapes of alcohol or other drugs. Patience is particularly important for both the pessimism (things will probably look better, later) and the sadness (see if it does not lift somewhat).

*At the same time, depression is a clear proof of the error in "Time will heal." Time in itself does not cure much in the emotional and mental stresses. Just as you can study yourself deeper into error, you can make yourself more and more melancholy with time.

*For time to heal, the mixture of depression needs the ingredient of *hope*. Call it what you like, the psychology of hope, the attitude of hope. What you need is a Probability of Success View, what we call our "POS View."

*Hope comes from seeing chances of success, likelihood of improvement. Or more accurately, *probability* of good outcomes in whatever you feel depressed about: love relationships, job, personal attainments. Probability guides our lives and depressions. If you are depressed, it is mainly in your probability view. Your probability view is your expectation — of what you are thinking will happen. Try to raise your view of the likelihood of good outcomes.

*You can raise your probability-of-success view both by recalling your past achievements and by reviewing your skills.

*You can best raise your POS View, however, by action: by doing something. Life has a wonderful way of being therapeutic, as long as we *do* something.

*If your probability of success view does not change by your own efforts, it is a good sign that you will be better helped by seeing a mental health professional. At least, your own effort will have achieved this: you are now *motivated* to do something about your depression.

Let me conclude this very important topic by saying that depression is a very complicated distress. Depression is, not a single mood state, but any of a number of states and outlooks. It can be a pessimism (as we have seen) about one's self, world, friends; or about one's past, future or even present. It can be a sense of failure, either personal or social. It can be the experience of a total lack of rewarding events or satisfactions. It can be an intense state of the guilt, shame and fear which were discussed earlier. And of course, depression can have very pronounced biochemical sources. In sum, depression can be many things and so it is terribly hard to come up with a single solution which might help every depressed person. It is called the "common cold" of mental problems —and we all know how diverse are a cold's remedies!

For the same reason, I would suggest that you be very cautious about trying to rely totally on yourself if your depression is at all intense and discomforting. Particularly if you find that you are so uncomfortable as to be unable to manage your daily affairs and responsibilities, this is probably a clear sign that you will be well-advised to find professional help. Neither the "bootstrap" approach (I'll pick myself up) nor the kindly neighbor's listening are likely to be sufficient if your depression is intense. The good news is that today there are some very effective professional approaches waiting to help you in your depression.

Chapter Seven

Preparing for Your Unique Stress: Death and the Rest

THREE VULNERABILITIES

Is there any way that a person may prepare for an upcoming stress?

You set aside a moment of calm, fully convinced that preparation is all important. You are convinced that your best learned skills are those learned in quiet. Future stress there will be — that you know. But, you also know that stress is a very personal affair. So many of our stresses are unique to you. Some stressors which disturb others greatly may not faze you at all. Equally, other stressors are very troublesome to you though you may notice other people write them off as "no problem."

> Ted and Fred are brothers who are partners in an appliance business. They are in a competitive line of work because so much profit depends on trade-ins, which in turn must be resold. They must live with this most noticeable fact: the high risks involved prices they offer for traded appliances. Ted finds it a challenging business. To Fred it is agonizingly stressful and he is continually upset.

> Jill and Jim are divorcing. While divorce is admittedly hard on anyone, Jim experiences more stress than Jill, being more confused and anxious and quite at a loss on how to cope with being single.

Fred and Jim have weak spots, an achilles heel, which they could strengthen if they knew how.

I'm Doing My Best... But It Isn't Enough

Each person has some weak spots which predispose him or her to their own unique stresses. Knowing what your weak spots are is a first step toward developing a life style for coping with stress. Knowing how to prepare for your own stresses also helps you appreciate why some things which work for others in stress may not be working for you. But it also enables you to zero in on what will work for you, though it may not work for others.

What makes a threat become a stress for you? You will be able to anticipate advice you have heard: "Well, it all depends...." Depends on *what*, you prod. Too often much of the advice then trails away into obvious and perhaps innocuous comments on differences between people in age, sex, education — none of which are very helpful. The Freds and Jims in life need something more specific.

You have three potential weak spots to look into when preparing for future stresses. Richard Lazarus, who has researched for years what our personality brings to stress, has identified these three vulnerability areas:

*Needs that are high
*Beliefs that are strong
*Resources that are weak

Knowing these vulnerabilities we will be able to prepare, in this chapter, for such stresses as: death; injury and illness;

To begin these vulnerabilities we can "jump in feet first," if you please, into the stress of facing the threat of death. This obvious stress will reveal vividly how any stress affects people differently, especially in their needs and motives.

THE DISTRESS OF DEATH

Would the threat of an imminent death be a stress for you?

What a question to ask! Of course it would, you will probably answer. Yet even with this, in some way the ultimate threat, death, is a stress of varying degrees. A priest friend of mine told me a two-part story which points out how differing a stress death can be for two persons. The priest, Father Ray, once visited a man in the hospital who was dying of cancer.

The priest approached him to see if he wanted to talk. Not at all, the man applied. On later visits Father Ray stopped by, if only to chat. The man, his health deteriorating, with no visitors, rigid in his attitude, showed his anger and would have nothing to do with the priest. Eventually the man was near death. The priest came in his room, again cordially, but was met with these words, "Listen, I'm only forty. I've made a lot of plans but now I'll get to do none of them. I once was a Catholic but that stuff is nonsense. I'm angry as hell; in fact, if there is a hell I wish I could take you with me to it." It did not take him long to die — angry, alone and frustrated.

On another occasion the same priest visited the hospital where a ten year old child was sick, also soon to die because of a serious bone disease. Once they had become friendly, the priest and the boy spoke openly about approaching death. Asked if he were scared of dying, the boy said that at first he was, "But now I'm not because I think more about going to heaven. My family visits me every day and we talk about it and what it will be like." Then the boy added, "Father Ray, I wish I could take you with me." The priest found that the dying statement of the two, so similar yet so different, haunted him afterwards.

Death's differing stress. To the child, death meant going to a place where he expected to be happy. To the adult, death meant the possibility of a life "hereafter" none too comfortable. Quite aside from whose view you might select as "correct," if either, these two persons facing the same dreaded event show a profound truth about any stress. *Stress is in the eye of the beholder, to some important degree.* What is in the "eye" of the stress beholder is the person's view of his/her needs, resources, and beliefs.

We assume at least implicitly that the threat to remaining alive is a universal and equal stress to all persons. We assume that wanting to remain alive is universal and equal in all. Yet death is a stress of varying degrees to different people. The pivotal question is, *What makes death a threat?* and it is answered far more differently than one might suppose.

To some people death is a stress which is unbearable; to most people death is quite severe though not unbearable; to still others it is tolerable; and to others it is welcome. Death differs in stress to the astronaut, the firefighter, the parent, the lonely widow, the teenager, the career soldier, the skydiving stuntman or the forty year old woman with a fledgling business. It all depends upon the person's needs, resources, and beliefs. These are the three vulnerabilities to death as a stress.

The man had many needs which he saw would not be satisfied, many goals unachieved. The child saw "heaven" as a place for his needs to be satisfied. The man was alone, without much of social resources; the boy had his family and friends to support him. They also had differing beliefs and attitudes toward death.

Needs in death. Our patterns of motives are involved in stress. To appreciate the significance of death we must first consider a person's need system. Particularly important are a person's needs for achievement, affiliation, autonomy, and dominance. The child was obviously low on these needs and felt that other needs for happiness would be satisfied in dying — thus, low stress. The man very likely was high on most of these needs, so death was high stress.

Needs are the first area of vulnerabilities. If we are going to prepare for an upcoming stress like death we will have to understand its importance and assess our own needs.

Briefly, the first rule of thumb in anticipating stress for you is this: *if a need is high, a threat to that need will become a stress.* Stress, in short, is a strong threat to a high need. So a strong need or motive will be the first clue to you of where your own stresses will be in the future. Stress invariably turns out to be a threat to our greatest desires and motivations.

At once you can notice something very positive about this. Stress is very often your greatest discloser to yourself of what your own values and needs really are. They may not be very clear to you until you think about death, for example, but then under the threat the needs become urgent. A fireman once told me that, facing death so often, he *has* to make up his mind early about what he is living and dying for. Stress is so intertwined with one's patterns of motives that these motives may only be felt and struggled for in a time of stress. Likewise a person going through a divorce said she never realized how important her need for intimacy was until she was stressed with the decision to separate.

Attitudes in dying. The stress of death, like any stress, is not limited to our needs and patterns of motives. The attitudes and beliefs we hold also make us more or less vulnerable to special stresses. In death the meaning is different for various people. Attitudes toward death may vary as researcher Feifel has found: "To many, death represents the teacher of transcendental truth incomprehensible during life. For others, death is a friend who brings an end to pain through peaceful sleep. Then there are those who see it as the great destroyer who is to be fought to the bitter end." It is all a matter of attitude, or meaning and belief.

The child mentioned earlier had a clear belief that death meant "going to heaven," whereas the man seemed to hold an attitude that death is indeed the great destroyer. Attitudes are those general beliefs and opinions we hold about life and death. We are today prone to some stresses precisely because of our attitudes: they guide our interpretations about what happens and what we can do.

The second law of stress is this: *The more ambiguous the threats the more important are attitudes or belief systems in determining how we will cope.* Our attitudes are our working belief systems. They are our generalizations which dispose us to act and guide those actions.

Attitudes in stress also show in another way how we do not enter our problems alone. We depend on people. We come to our stress with social, cultural beliefs. Death, for example is not only seen as a stress according to our needs but also according to our attitudes toward it and these come from our culture, religion and other social institutions. Death may mean an end, a "cessation," or a road to a hereafter, a reunion with loved ones. Japanese cultural beliefs probably play a large role in giving, at one time, that country one of the highest suicide rates in the world. Likewise the high suicide rate in Sweden and Denmark seems traceable to attitudes of suicide being more acceptable than, for exmaple, in Norway.

Resources in death. The third and final area of vulnerability is the resources we have in facing the threat of death or any threat. Who can we turn to? Can we rely on family and friends to see us through the threat? In facing death, are there agencies and helpers to help us prepare or who are going

I'm Doing My Best . . . But It Isn't Enough

through the same thing? If we cannot see any resources, the stress will be greater.

The third rule of thumb is: *A person who can cope successfully knows where his or her resources are.* In the stress of dying, some people turn to religion as a resource. Attitudes again determine where we see our resources to be. But we need to find resources somewhere: in friends, professionals, family. But most of all we must find resources in ourselves: in our fond memories of family and friends, recollections of achievements we have made, trips we have taken and experiences we have had. Particularly important for coping with stresses, then, are our "mental resources."

A person with difficulties is almost by definition a person who has no resources or does not know where his or her resources are. Stresses produce disorganization in us, as we have seen. That disorgnization may mean precisely that we do not know where to go for help. To feel vulnerable is to feel without resources — and to be stressed. It is this simple: stress is to be without resources.

There are three kinds of resources we need to recognize and be able to assess in preparing for upcoming stresses. First, there are the resources within ourselves. Second there are the resources in other people we know and can already depend upon. Third, there are resources in our social and civic community: the agencies, financial aid, and public networks of help. We have already spoken of these three resources in Chapter Two. Further practical advice will be given in Chapter Ten.

A CLOSER LOOK AT THREE WEAKNESSES

First Vulnerability: Assessing Our Needs

> *People who are prone to the stress of being overworked, Overload Stress, usually have a high need for achievement plus a few other needs.

> *People who are prone to the stress of Burnout often have high needs for being socially recognized and need achievement, plus a few more.

*People who are prone to the stress of Competition also usually have a high need for achievement but also a low self concept (though this sounds strange).

*People who are prone to the stress of feeling pained at being rejected by others have high needs for social approval and for being included, plus a few more needs.

*People who are prone to the stress of Uncontrol have a high need for Control in their own lives, plus a few more needs such as a low need for dependence upon others.

*People who are prone to the stress of Boredom have a high need for stimulation or challenge, a low need for routine, and probably have a low self concept.

If you now turn to Figure 7-2 you will see a variety of predictable stresses and their counterpart vulnerabilities: needs, resources, and working beliefs. Look now more closely at the first needs.

We have seen that the first rule of thumb in anticipating your own personal stresses is this: If the need is high, a threat to that need will become a stress. Stress is precisely a strong threat to a high need. Your first order of business is to assess your needs.

Assessing how high are your needs can be a simple matter or as complex as you want it to be. You will be given an opportunity to assess *your* own needs as we proceed, and thus to prepare for your own stresses. But to cope with stress requires, first to last, that you see your own motives and their patterns are not quite the motives of another person. Stress is very personal that way. Recall Jim and Jill going through their divorce and remember Fred and Ted in their competitive business. These four people had different needs, and thus differing stresses. But the threat of death or injury may be the clearest place to start the practical steps of assessing our own personal, special needs.

To appreciate the significance of death, we must consider a person's need system, including his or her needs for achievement, affiliation, and autonomy. These are the first area of a person's three vulnerabilities. If we are going to prepare for upcoming stresses, we must assess what our needs are.

Figure 7-2

If You Find Your Stress Is | **Then You Are Vulnerable In**
($*$ = major difficulty)

1. Overload
Need: to achieve and to be approved
**Resources Unused:* your own time; other people
Attitude: Perfectionism; personal control

2. Competition
Need: to achieve
Resources Unused: skills of cooperation
**Attitude:* Succeed by beating others

3. Burnout
Need: to be appreciated, approved by others
**Resources Unused:* personal satisfactions colleagues support
Attitude: exaggerated expectations of others

4. Boredom
Need: Curiosity; self esteem
Resources: opportunities around you
**Attitude:* negative, limited view of self

5. Loneliness
Need: affiliation, intimacy
**Resources Unused:* personal social skills, agencies, situations in your community
**Attitude:* Belief others must take the initiative

How *do* we assess our needs? Remaining with the stress of death will be our clue. The general picture of death is that it is stressful because *consequences* are *feared*. In addition, the fears that a person has most intensely are related to the role a person has or expected to have. Death means different levels of stress to different persons because of their personal needs: their needs are disclosed by the consequences, for them personally, of death. Death can be a teacher, a friend, a great destroyer, a means of vengeance to others, a means of punishment and atonement for oneself.

Feifel has identified a common theme which spells out a consequence most feared. The stress of death is not in the event of death itself but in what is *feared*: "waste of limited years, unassayed tasks, locked opportunities, the talents withering in disuse, the avoidable evils which have been done."

We must first look at the fears of consequences we have in any upcoming stress — this is the first practical thing to do in preparing for stress.

FEARS IN STRESSES

Briefly it amounts to assessing your conscious fears. That is, a need is perhaps best recognized by its absence in our lives. The absence of a need tells us exactly what bearing this stressful situation would have in our own lives. The fear is the degree to which we see something as being required. Let us return to our needs and death.

Fear of Death. What, for you would be some consequences of death right now? Suppose you knew you would die in the coming week. What would you most fear? Put a check beside any of the following actual statements made by others:

"I FEAR:"	WHICH TELLS ME I HAVE A HIGH NEED OF:
___ 1. I would have no more experience	Exploration
___ 2. I am uncertain as to what might happen to me if there is life after death	Certainty/Clarity
___ 3. I am afraid of what might happen to my body after death.	Control
___ 4. I could no longer care for my dependents.	Nourish others
___ 5. All my plans and projects would come to an end.	Control/Competency
___ 6. My death would cause grief to my relatives.	Independence
___ 7. The process of dying might be painful.	Safety
___ 8. Other _____	_____

I'm Doing My Best ... But It Isn't Enough

To repeat, in preparing for those events which will be genuinely stressful to you, perhaps uniquely to you, you should begin by assessing your needs at the present time. You have begun by assessing your needs, through your fears, of the most threatening of all stresses — death. Understandably death engages more fears and therefore more needs than any other stress. But the same logic applies to other stress possibilities: *examine your greatest fears and you will see your greatest needs or motives,* in reverse.

SECOND VULNERABILITY: RESOURCES

*People going through a divorce find it helpful to be with others going through the same experience.

*People who have problems with drinking and other addictions find it helpful to be with others like themselves.

*Workers who are suffering overload distresses are helped by having bull-sessions and other sharing conversations with people in the same situation.

*People who are injured or handicapped gain much strength by sharing with others with similar distresses.

If death is a distress disclosing one's first vulnerability, needs, then any moment of feeling helpless or uninformed will clearly remind you of the second vulnerability: your resources — or lack of them.

The above situations illustrate a major resource in stress and distress: other people. One does not feel so helpless when with others; nor does one feel so adrift or uninformed if others are going through the same thing. People coping with other people vividly demonstrate the truth in the saying (mentioned earlier): "We didn't come over in the same ship but we are all in the same boat."

To be resourceful is to be able to cope. Thus the second rule of coping is this: a person who copes successfully *knows* where his/her resources are. Hold onto that word "knows." I would like to indicate something terribly important about the above instances of people being with other people. There is abundant evidence now of why people want to get together in times of stress and distress. Getting together satisfies a very important, if unrecognized, *need*: the need to know yourself.

When you want to get together in your distress you should recognize that it is for needs other than support and reassurance. There is another need which appears to be even more important: the need for self-knowledge.

Much of the time you will be able to understand yourself only through being with other people. What happens is that in stress and distress you are constantly *comparing* yourself to others. And this comparing that goes on is very helpful, even strengthening to you. What precisely are you comparing in yourself and others? The answer seems to be a comparison of three parts of your personality: your feelings, your opinions, and your abilities.

You want to *know*, through others, how intense and appropriate are your feelings of worry, sadness, guilt and all the rest. But you also want to *know*, by talking to others, whether your opinions about your dilemma are accurate, and whether you have looked at all the alternatives. Finally, you want to *know*, by observing others, whether you are skilled enough to deal with your situation. So, getting together with others has much to do with knowing where your resources are.

The other side of the coin points to one's vulnerability about resources. Richard Lazarus put the matter succinctly: "The dull or uninformed probably perceives himself to be more vulnerable to danger." In extreme, being out of contact or having mental limitations makes a person more vulnerable to stress and distress.

But then — when facing a dilemma and many distresses, who among us does not at the time feel "dull and uninformed." It is the very nature of stress to present a person with the ambiguous. It is the first feature of distress to leave one confused. You do not feel very smart when overworked, depressed, laid off, divorced, or overlooked by your fellow human beings.

But the second rule for decoding what stresses you are proned to remains: a person is more vulnerable to those stresses where he does not know his resources. Stress and distress produce disorganization. That disorganization means in your situation that you do not know where to go for help. To feel vulnerable means you do not know where to go for help.

I'm Doing My Best . . . But It Isn't Enough 153

You, in the theme of a dilemma, "don't know where to turn." To feel vulnerable is to feel without resources — and thus to be distressed. It is that simple.

The moral is to know the resources you will need in your own dilemma. Recall what you did in the sixth question of your decision making Chapter Five: Can I find a new option, one I did not see before? And so you went to two new people and then to some special organization which is particularly informed about your problem, whether it be finding a job, divorce, re-locating, settling work disputes, and so on. Know your resources.

THIRD VULNERABILITY: ATTITUDES AND WORKING BELIEFS

The stress of death clearly illustrates our first vulnerability, needs. Feeling stupid illustrates our second vulnerability, resources. Another vulnerability is pointed up, curiously but clearly, by *boredom*.

Consider the stress of Bored Bosco. He is filled with apathy since becoming an insurance agent. He lives with the fear of being a failure, since not being accepted into law school years ago. Now his life is tedious. He sees himself as a poor husband and father, thinks of himself as being alone at work since he travels by himself most of the time. He is bored.

Boredom is a special kind of fatigue. Not the kind of fatigue which comes from physical, objective hard work such as working in the garden, painting the house, carrying freight and so on. Boredom is a subjective fatigue and it does not go away. Boredom really is a state of mind, a matter of *attitude toward oneself*. Bored Bosco's fatigue is different from regular fatigue in three ways. First it is a feeling which is continual and long standing, whereas normal physical fatigue is somewhat temporary. Second, Bosco's fatigue is not lessened by rest or sleep; rather, he sleeps most of the weekend but feels no better on Monday morning. Thirdly, if an emergency arises or he gets an unexpected chance to play golf on a course he has dreamed of, his fatigue disappears for a while; this is not one of physical fatigue. Bosco's fatigue is one of an attitude.

Today his psychological fatigue appears in talking about *"Burnout."* Though Burnout is talked about as something new, it has been with us a rather long time — under less trendy names. Solutions for Burnout are probably best found in Attitude solutions, coupled with regaining one's strengths. That is: the solution is in changing one's attitude (discussed in the next chapter) and exploring more of one's resources.

"A bore is someone who never seems to have a previous engagement," a wit has said. The witticism may be one part attitude. Bored Boscoes are often people who simply do not find anything meaningful, nothing of a "previous engagement." Their boredom is precisely due to lacking previous concerns. Their boredom is due to lack of interests, attitudes. The attitude involved in boredom is this: *a negative feeling state which is a negative evaluation of oneself and one's ability.*

The point about boredom is that we are prone to certain stresses because of our attitudes or general beliefs. Attitudes are our general opinions about life. Attitudes guide our interpretations of what happens to us and what we can do.

Before we look at special attitudes which may dispose us to particular stresses we should know what they are — and are not. Attitudes are a bit more general than needs mentioned heretofore. Attitudes are closer to being our practical working "philosophy of life."

Much of stress today comes from our attitudes. Stress accelerates as demands and needs become unclear. The third rule of preparing for stress is this: *the more ambiguous the threats, the more important will be our attitudes and belief systems in determining how we will cope.* Our attitudes are our working belief system. Attitudes are generalizations which dispose us to act and guide our behavior.

If there is one thing clear from how stress and distress affect people it is that a person's attitudes prevent or foster effective coping. "He who is too old to learn was probably always too old to learn," is a fair description of how an attitude can hold a person back. Just as needs can be changed, and often must be changed, so too with attitudes.

Attitudes are our working beliefs and they guide us in interpreting our life experiences.

Attitudes and experience. Attitudes are a person's working beliefs and guide that person in interpreting his/her experiences. These attitudes make one pause over the

I'm Doing My Best... But It Isn't Enough

saying, "We learn by experience." This is not so much true as a half-truth. If experience were such a good teacher, everyone would be a good decision maker; we saw in Chapter Five this is a questionable assumption. If people always learn by experience you would not find people making the same mistakes over and over again: divorce after divorce, job loss after job loss. People who are rolling-stones fail to prove that experience, in itself, is much of a teacher at all. Reflection leads to a more seasoned principle: *What we learn from experience pretty much depends upon the beliefs and attitudes we take into the experience.*

The next chapter continues with attitudes which affect stress and distress. Some of the most predictable of stresses are those which are very much a result of attitudes.

In summary, preparing for stresses which are personal and particular for *you* means looking at your "life style." That life style includes at the very least these three factors: your needs, your attitudes, and your resources. These are the essentials to look at though there are other things too. For example, your behavior patterns contribute to stresses. But if you look closely at what your needs, attitudes and resources are, you will find you can then take some actions which will help you cope with your own particular stresses.

You probably already have a fairly good idea of what is stressful and distressful to you. Commonly experienced distresses include being overworked, in a competitive "rat-race" or jungle (as it is diversely called), feeling run over by others or held back. Read on, into the next two chapters. Before doing so you may want to go over Figure 7-2 again to see what your own life style factors are: what three achilles heels you have.

Chapter Eight

Distresses Predictable From Your Own Attitudes: Overload and Competition

In Chapter Seven we learned how to prepare for distresses which may be unique to us. We saw that in moments of calm we should attend to three vulnerabilities: our needs, resources and belief systems. These each make us prone to particular distresses.

There are common, predictable distresses and such are the concern of this chapter. We each experience these common, predictable distresses in our own personal way. Our needs, resources and personal attitudes bring us to the point of being susceptible to the following predictable distresses:

Over-Work and Burnout Distresses
Competition Distress

We will here examine each of these distresses. But now we are armed with the equipment coming from Chapter Seven, equipment we can now develop. As we spell out some practical steps to take for each of these distresses, we will be able to strengthen ourselves in the three areas of our needs, resources, and attitudes or beliefs. Sometimes this "strengthening" will entail correcting an attitude or changing a need, as well as enhancing our resources. You may already suspect which of the above distresses is predictable for *you*. You will here have a chance to understand it more fully as well as develop more skills to cope with.

I'm Doing My Best . . . But It Isn't Enough 157

These distresses are predictable and, I must add, they are also attackable. There are definite ways of attacking them and dealing with them. But first we must see why they are so predictable in certain people. For example, some persons are clear candidates for over-work distress and burn-out. They have a need which sets them up for distress, a very special need, which we must see in actual distress situations. Nowhere perhaps is overwork so likely, for example, as with a home-maker. The sheer work of keeping up a house, budgeting, car pooling, PTA meetings, attending activities of children from swimming to dance to scouts, shopping, and on and on. When so many responsibilities are attempted thoroughly, overwork and burn-out are a hazard written into the situation. The home-maker wife, and today more often the husband, can accentuate the distress by a particular need: the need to be "super-Mom," the perfect home-maker.

Let's look at such predictable distresses in another situation, that of business, for two persons, Helen and George in Figure 8-1.

Figure 8-1

OVERLOAD AND COMPETITIVE DISTRESS

Helen and George are two middle managers in a vast international corporation which produces electronic equipment. The most noteworthy feature of their work is meeting recurring deadlines. They face continual deadlines for proposals, sales reports. Every day has its deadlines, each of which hold out threats (and thus distress) for performance and decision. To whom will this distress be greater?

George will experience the threats more intensely: he has a high need for doing excellent work. He has proven over his 15 years with the company to be a producer. But he sees himself as needing more time, to be thorough and make calm careful preparations. He feels the need to maintain this image of

an excellent producer, to himself as well as others. George is finding the work more and more distressful. He is continually anxious, has developed an ulcer. Because he has such a reputation, other employees turn to him and he takes on still more work.
George has *Overload Distress.*

Helen has another kind of distress. She says, "I work best under pressure. I'm very competitive. I thrive on deadlines." Helen seems to be coping well enough, though her blood pressure has gone up recently, and she has put on some extra weight. Helen smokes more. She remains out to "prove" how much higher in the organization she can go; she secretly wants to do this by doing better than George.

George and Helen show how predictable distresses are, and why. Each has differing needs, uses resources differently, and holds certain attitudes — distress factors we discussed in Chapter Seven. But there is more. Some people, in their personalities, make predictable distresses very predictable indeed. That one other factor is their *self-image.* Persons suffer distresses like Overload, Burn-out, Failure, Type A, Competition, and the like because of their self-image. For your own predictable distresses, you too must return to your self.

YOUR SELF PREDICTS YOUR DISTRESS

Your self-image is your most valuable resource. Your self-image is closely connected with your *need* for self esteem. We separate this need from all other needs mentioned earlier because it is so special. *Your self-image and self esteem, you will find, is not only part of the problem, but the major part of the solution.* Your Self is your major handle, strength and coping technique — once you learn how to apply this Self to distress.

As you enter any task, approach any threat, cope with any distress your Self is "on the make," if you please. Your self-

I'm Doing My Best ... But It Isn't Enough **159**

image is up to one of three things. Either you are out to *improve* and enhance your image, as does Helen. Or, you are out to maintain your image, as does George. Or, you may be out to do something entirely different: to *evaluate* and understand yourself. You will of course do all three things at a given time, but mainly you do one of the three more than the other two.

THREE KINDS OF SELF-IMAGES

One thoughtful expert, Albert Pepitone, has offered a splendid framework on how to make sense about your self based needs in distress. He has observed that in distress there are actually these three self-based needs at work: the need to enlarge and enhance, the need to maintain or "validate," and the need to evaluate and understand.

Begin now with a little experience. Take a piece of paper and write at the top of that page, *Who Am I?* Then below it write down the answer, any answer that comes to your mind. After that answer the question a second time. Answer it still a third time, and continue until you have given nine answers to that single question. This should tell you how *clear* you are about your self-image.

Now try another experience. Ask yourself whether you have tried any of the following experiences.

*I have tried a new hobby in the past six months.
*I have changed my view on an important (political, personal, professional) issue.
*I actively listened (as described in Chapter Two) to a political, religious, professional or personal viewpoint different from my own for fifteen minutes.
*Though I see myself as a leader, I deliberately took on the role of a follower for one full hour on a task.
*Though I see myself as a follower, I deliberately took the role of a leader for one full hour on a task.

This will tell you how *changeable* you see yourself.

From these two experiences you should be able to check one (and only one) of the following statements as being true of *you most of the time.*

*1) I am the kind of person who is clear about my self-image and mainly see myself as unchangeable.
*2) I am the kind of person who is clear about my self-image and mainly see myself also as being able to change.
*3) I am the kind of person who is unclear about my self-image but mainly see myself also being able to change.

Persons who check #1 are *Self-Maintainers*. They are mainly interested in "validating" their present self-image. If you checked this you are probably chiefly interested in showing who you are, what you have become. Your self-image is clear, certain, and unchanging. Persons like you find distress particularly when there is much rapid change. Your predictable distress will be when you have to acquire new skills, make rather large adjustments or present yourself in a new way.

Consistency and continuity are important satisfactions to you, since they meet your self-need of maintaining your view of yourself. You are like George whose major threats, or distresses, involve rapid change.

Persons who check #2 have a marked tendency to want to enlarge and improve themselves. If you checked this your self-image is to be competitive, to achieve much and to take a lot of risks. You are a *Self-Enhancer* most of the time. Distresses which are particularly bothersome to you are of two types. On the one hand, you will be extremely upset with boredom, sameness and ruts of all kinds; and you will seek novelty and extra excitement. On the other hand, you run the risks of making "competition" your main incentive, are easily misled by it so that it does harm to your relationships with people, your cooperativeness, and you become a prize candidate for heart problems. You are like the Helens of life, and your predictable distress is one called a Type A or cardiac condition.

Suppose you checked #3. Then you are neither a Helen or a George. Instead, you are a *Self-Aware* person. Your main needs are to understand yourself, to evaluate yourself. You have a self-image of one who is unclear about yourself but who also wants both to become more clear and to change or

I'm Doing My Best... But It Isn't Enough

grow. You mainly see the need for other people in your life, to help you understand yourself and to grow in helpful ways. So, your self-image moves you to want to be with other people and to cooperate with them. Your main distresses, therefore, will be situations of harsh rivalry where it is "dog-eat-dog" competition. Equally upsetting to you will be circumstances of bland monotony. You, like Self-Enhancers, feel that contentment is for cows. But unlike the persons who checked #1, you feel that cooperation, sharing and supporting is a better way to change, grow and become more aware of yourself.

OVERVIEW OF COPING WITH PREDICTABLE DISTRESSES

Now that we have seen the three kinds of Self-images, we know what people get into their own predictable distresses. We can now put this together with the Three Vulnerabilities spoken of earlier, to identify what the problems are for each kind of distress. If you look at Figure 8-2, you will see what are the vulnerabilities for each distress.

To formulate a plan to cope with any of these distresses, you must cope with short-order-solutions and long-term-solutions. Briefly this means your "attack" on these distresses are of two kinds:

*ACTIONS TO TAKE — Short-Order-Solutions
*ATTITUDES TO SHAPE — Long-Term-Solutions

The first are short order solutions, the latter are long term solutions. The first are SOS responses directed at your present level of functioning, the second are directed at the underlying cause of your distress, your style of life.

Actions to take. These are the five steps introduced in Chapter Three.

    1) GET IT OUT: Talk to a good listener
    2) GET A HANDLE: Put the distress in a structure of Conflict or Frustration
    3) GET RID OF RIGIDITY: Do an active form of relaxation
    4) SHORE UP RESOURCES
    5) GET AN ACTION PLAN

Figure 8-2

THE STRESS OF:	VULNERABILITIES:
OVERWORK	NEED TO BE ALTERED: ACHIEVEMENT RESOURCES: OTHERS USED TOO LITTLE SELF TENDENCIES OVER-USED SELF-MAINTAINING ATTITUDE: PERFECTIONISM
TYPE A CARDIAC	NEED: ACHIEVEMENT RESOURCES: SELF ENHANCING TENDENCY DOMINATES ALL ATTITUDE: PERFECTIONISM AND COMPETITIVENESS AS VALUES
BOREDOM	NEED: FOR EXCITEMENT NOVELTY RESOURCES: UNDERUSED SELF: HELPED BY ASSERTIVENESS
REJECTION	NEED: FOR APPROVAL RESOURCES: INSUFFICIENT APPRECIATION OF PERSONAL WORTH ATTITUDE: COMPLIANCE, EXAGGERATED NEED OF OTHERS FOR SELF WORTH
BURN-OUT	NEED: ACHIEVEMENT AND APPROVAL RESOURCES: INSUFFICIENT USE OF INNER STRENGTHS ATTITUDE: PERFECTIONISM AND OF APPRECIATION

Attitudes to shape. This will be to examine your Life Style, which includes your three vulnerabilities of needs, resources and attitudes. In addition, you will need to examine your personal kind of self-image.

Coping with distress does not stop with assessing your life style, however. You have to change your life style. You must be prepared to change some of your attitudes, temper some of your expectations, alter some of your needs. Obviously, you have to see that these attitudes, expectations and needs *can* be changed. Seeing this changeableness in yourself is the "iffy" part, which you must accept. For this reason, to help you see you can change there are essays on particular vulnerable attitudes — included in the hope that they will help you look more probingly at your own problem attitudes. For the same reason, you may need professional help with your distress: that is, to see what attitudes you need to change and how to do it. The limits of a self-help book are often precisely here: how much can you change your lifestyle of attitudes, resources, needs and self-image. Often these cannot be changed by purely reading a book; they need the frequent added ingredient of "working through" with the guidance of a professional mental health worker.

"There is more to life than increasing its speed."

OVERLOAD DISTRESS

   *The problem need is Achievement
   *The self concept is The Perfection of a Self-Maintainer or Self-Enhancer
   *Resources: other people insufficiently used
   *The problem attitude: I must control, by doing everything perfectly myself.

Perhaps your predictable distress if overload. If you are in business you feel like George. Everyone says, "Let George do it!" You are overworked. Or if you are a home-maker, you feel that it is all too much: getting the plumbing fixed, going to the kids games and activities, car-pooling, shopping, the car washes and baking something for the fund raising drive. You want to be a "runaway."

Now is a good time to stop and assess if your predictable distress is Overload. The authors Girdano and Everly (1979) offer a useful exercise presented in Figure 8-3.

Figure 8-3

How often do you...

___ 1. Find yourself with insufficient time to complete your work?
      (a) Almost always   (b) Very often
      (c) Seldom   (d) Never

___ 2. Find yourself becoming confused and unable to think clearly because too many things are happening at once?
      (a) Almost always   (b) Very often
      (c) Seldom   (d) Never

___ 3. Wish you had help to get everything done?
      (a) Almost always   (b) Very often
      (c) Seldom   (d) Never

___ 4. Feel that people around you simply expect too much from you?
      (a) Almost always   (b) Very often
      (c) Seldom   (d) Never

___ 5. Feel overwhelmed by the demands placed upon you?
      (a) Almost always   (b) Very often
      (c) Seldom   (d) Never

___ 6. Find your work infringing upon your leisure hours?
      (a) Almost always   (b) Very often
      (c) Seldom   (d) Never

___ 7. Get depressed when you consider all of the tasks that need your attention?
      (a) Almost always   (b) Very often
      (c) Seldom   (d) Never

___ 8. See no end to the excessive demands placed upon you?
      (a) Almost always   (b) Very often
      (c) Seldom   (d) Never

___ 9. Have to skip a meal so that you can get work completed?
      (a) Almost always   (b) Very often
      (c) Seldom   (d) Never

___ 10. Feel that you have too much responsibility?
      (a) Almost always   (b) Very often
      (c) Seldom   (d) Never

Scoring: a=4, b=3, c=2, d=1   Score: _____

Self-Assessment Exercise 3 was designed to assess your level of stress due to overload. Total your points and see how stressed you are by overload. Roughly speaking, a total of 26 to 40 points is indicative of a high stress level; such an excessive level could be psychologically and physiologically debilitating if steps are not taken to reduce this level. A total of 20 to 25 points is indicative of moderate stress, and 10 to 19 points indicates low stress due to overload. You can get further insight into the specifics of overload stress by analyzing the specific items. Items 1, 2, 6, and 9 pertained to time demands placed upon you. Items 4, 5, 7, and 8 concerned expectations from superiors, family and self. Finally, items 3 and 10 looked at how much support you have in facing your stress. Are you disproportionately high or low in any of these areas?

COPING WITH OVERLOAD DISTRESS

Suppose you find that your score on overload Distress is high. The exercise may be telling you what you already suspected, but it can also tell you more. If you look back on your scores on specific items, you will notice these themes: that time demands are heavy on you, that you infrequently get support in your excessive workload, and most importantly that your distress is one of expectations — from self, family and colleagues. Your expectatons are at the heart of your distress.

You as a person in an Overload distress are dominated by expectations. Your expectations, in turn, are part of your high need to achieve. And so your distress of Overload tells you (a) what your high needs are; (b) what this means, what the implications are to have such a high need, and (c) what to do about this distress, both in attitudes to re-shape and actions to take.

George's Overload. The Overload distress discloses that you have a particularly high need for achievement. Now, most people share a moderate amount of this need. Most of us want to do a good job, even an excellent job by any standards. It is our motive for a special kind of satisfaction. This is a need which is our capacity to enjoy successful efforts. But this very need can create George's Overload.

George's Overload came from having barriers to doing excellent work. These barriers make a "frustration" of our efforts. The barriers may be from time limits, lack of support and help, or expectations — as indicated above. They stand in the way of doing what we want to do, having a "need" to do satisfactorily. We are frustrated, in the sense explained earlier. And that frustration is the distress you are now experiencing.

Coping with overload distress will take these two directions: first, briefly examining your Attitude Shape-up which includes looking at your needs, resources and beliefs; secondly, going over your steps to take.

Long Term Solutions

Lifestyles For Overload Distress

A. Briefly, your need which dominates your life is the need for achievement. Recognize at once your strength: you desire excellence. You are a highly motivated person. Your distress comes from what you set as goals, which are too high. You *can* lower these goals; you do this by lowering your expectations, for they bring on your distress. Your achilles heel is, strangely perhaps, your "perfectionism." Perfectionism is a goal you can reach only in very simple matters. Read the paragraphs below on perfectionism very carefully. Unless you are prepared to "shape up" your expectations here, your distress will continue.

B. Your resources are yourself, family, friends, and co-workers. You will need to get your concerns out in the open with them. You will also benefit by delegating more responsibility. Do not try to do everything nor, for the same reason, try to get all the glory. Two major ways to develop resourcefulness are discussed later: getting control of your life and time and creating a cooperative atmosphere with co-workers.

C. Attitudes or working belief systems of your probably include wanting too much control where little is possible.

An Essay On Perfect Achievements

Reshape The Achievement Need. One of the main difficulties in Overload distress is that today people have not been schooled in the art of genuine adaptiveness. What we have today is a lifestyle built around a simple-minded value, limitless achievement. An age of such achievement emphasis will automatically be an age of Overload distress. I need to explain this.

In both our work climates and citadels of higher education there is the theme: the need to succeed, to achieve, to perform well (or rather, better than everyone else) is the dominant value and motive. Now, suppose a young worker or student, so success-oriented, is induced to commit himself to performing in a situation that promises *failure*! What will happen to this person? Will he or she be shattered, disorganized and broken in spirit?

Precisely the above situation took place in a study by Cohen and Zimbardo (1969). Persons were induced for minimal rewards to work on a task that promised a high likelihood of failure. The result: their potent need to achieve success and avoid failure was significantly changed! They became less negative in feelings toward failing and they were less uncomfortable in the failure experience. That is, their general motivation to succeed had suffered a decrement.

The authors looked at the implications of this finding. If on the one hand you believe the high need for achievement is essential to the progress of civilization, you will not like the outcome. But on the other hand, if you see that you are driven by overachievement which has become a problem, then you may see, *"adjustment to failure is a vital part of the psychological development of any truly human being,"* say Cohen and Zimbardo.

Sometimes you have an overload distress because of a faulty learning: you have not learned to deal with failure! And this is to be deprived of a "vital part" of genuine human development. It is part of the skill of adaptive coping to be prepared for failures. Perhaps we should teach ourselves what Campbell and Stanley suggested for students: we must instill in them "the expectaton of tedium and disappointment and the duty of thorough persistence... We must expand our students' vow of poverty to include not only the willingness to accept poverty of finances, but also a poverty of experimental results." *What most people need to learn is, not how to be "winners," for this is easy; they need more to learn to deal with failures: to pick themselves up after falling down.*

The point of this is that, in our Overload distress, we *can change* our expectation; we can lower our achievement need — and by doing so we will at once experience less distress but also be developing the vital part of human development. This is our attitude toward achievement, an attitude which may be partly to blame for our distress: being too success oriented, too perfectionistic.

Perfectionism Pitfalls. It may sound strange, particularly to you who have a high need to achieve excellence, but you can indeed be too perfectionistic for your own good. One salesman prided himself in being a perfectionist not only in his work but as he coached little league football, which is very significant for two reasons. First, you can afford to be a perfectionist when things are simple and clear, as when a person misses a blocking assignment or makes it or stands just right while lining up. The pitfall of this is that few areas of life permit the luxury of being a perfectionist. Most areas do not permit simple, safe and perfect solutions. Perfectionism is for neat, black and white issues. But in most of living there are too many gray areas which do not admit of a *perfect* outcome.

It takes the most "gray matter" to work in gray areas.

Secondly, the attitude of perfectionism that an Overload person has spreads over to the rest of his life, as the salesman's did to little league football. Perhaps your work does permit perfectionistic following of company policies or producing the clear, if hard, outcome of gross income. If you spread that to the rest of your life, you will create all the problems of insisting that your home be always neat and tidy. You will create resentment in your spouse and children, much like retired military persons who insist "this home's going to be run like a tight ship," which ends making for severely troubled children who, though they may be "polite," grow both more apathetic and hostile. Similarly in this perfectionistic home, the atmosphere is never relaxed. The perfectionist is not "human" enough to be a partner, companion or parent. What works at work does not work at home.

But there is a third pitfall of perfectionism: rigidity. As we discussed in Chapter Three, rigidity is the main enemy of coping with distress and crisis. Most persons who cope well

I'm Doing My Best . . . But It Isn't Enough

have a flexibility, whereas poor copers are rigid. If you look closely at Figure 8-7, you will see the difference between rigidity and appropriate flexible coping.

SUPPOSE YOUR DISTRESS IS NEED FOR ACHIEVEMENT, THE DISTRESS: FAILURE

You have a high need for experiencing success. This makes you vulnerable to failure: you have a deep fear of failure.

Long Term Solutions

Actions you can take.

1. Visualize where it is you want success: some project at work, improvement at home, activity in your private life.

2. Now, spell out what would be "success" there:
    *raise at work, in salary
    *promotion?
    *award, signifying the approval of others
    *beating someone else out
    *being elected to some position

    OR

    *excellence of work projects itself — regardless of whether others pay, praise, applaud or promote you
    *features of the project: longer; more accurate; new features; comprehensive; well-presented

3. Put a likelihood of success figure: 10%, 50%, 90%. Be realistic because this is the tough part: you may find you are pursuing an "impossible dream:" 1% likely!

4. If you find that you are *too* prone to achievement needs, undertake something where you are most likely to fail: play tennis with a much better player. Try to meet an impossible quota: see, you can fail and still be okay, loved. Notice that this can lead you to CHANGE this motive.

Attitudes to shape.

1. Achievement and competence mean measuring yourself to some *standard*: Is yours to do something worthwhile in itself or to put someone down?

2. The achievement based on competition, putting others down, will invariable get you in the neck: LOOK CLOSELY AT ATTITUDES OF COMPETITION:
   a. Practically, what your business needs more is cooperation rather than competition.
   b. Personally, it develops a sickness of hostility; crippling effect on your children.

3. Go on to Helen's Distress: it has some pointers about competition and the constant tendency to compare yourself with others — all of which you should know.

THE DISTRESS OF COMPETITIVENESS: HELEN THE TYPE A

Now we can turn to Helen and all the competitive personalities — who have distresses of their own.

We can easily document the great value many people place on self worth through "self-enlargement," that is through getting Bigger and More (wealth, power, celebrity status). From elementary school to college, from little league to the junior chamber of commerce the need proclaimed is the same: succeed, yes, but mainly by outdoing the biggest and best — the enlarged. *Achieve* the Big. Self-worth is thus success by enlargement.

Then the notion of achieving takes a curious but all-important turn. To achieve really means to perform or gain *better* than everyone else. So achievement is equal with competition, and competition has value only for the one who "beats" others (eats their lunch, the saying goes) and comes out the Winner. As night follows the day, the slogan for life then becomes: "Winning is not the main thing, it's the only thing."

Thus does competition, on the wings of achievement, become as American as the flag. To doubt the value of competition is seen to strike at an *attitude* most central to American style of life, of experiencing success, of gaining self-worth. Still, to aid efforts at coping with distress this attitude toward competition must be examined — closely.

The distress involved is that of a personality Type A. This kind of person has recently become widely recognized thanks to the work of two cardiologists, Myer Friedman and Ray Rosenman. They found that coronary prone individuals are particularly likely to be in a threat because of achievement and competitive needs — the Helens of the world.

Competition Distress. "It's a jungle out there. It's dog-eat-dog competition." So true; competition is one fact which discloses how vulnerable we all are to distress.

Most people surely do live with competitive distresses: between businesses, within organizations for getting jobs and promotions, for getting into schools and training programs, for making sales, meeting quotas, attracting clients, and on and on. The threat of competition is so enormous in itself today as to make our age truly "an age of distress." Competition must be understood, for our own health, well-being and growth. Let us get to some facts briefly.

Fact one: competition is a universal experience of life.

Fact two: it is also true that under certain circumstances, we need competition; only under competition will we sometimes do our best.

Fact three: it is also true that we sometimes *seek* competition, therefore. The friendly game of tennis, checkers, cards, are clear evidence that the distress of competition is healthy and invigorating and is a big reason for us thinking there is "good distress" (eustress).

Fact four: still, nothing is so exaggerated as the value of competition. To profit from distress we have to be *suited* for it.

Limits to the value of competition. Competition is bearable, not to say healthy, only if we see the limits to its value. The first thing to do about competition is to examine our attitude about it. We can lessen the negative distress by examining how accurate our attitude is. The best way to examine our attitude is to start with the proverbs on that attitude, such as "It's a jungle out there."

The Jungle Image of life is true sometimes, but at others it is an outright misrepresentation of real life as we live it. The Jungle Image is true: when you buy products and services. There are dishonest sales persons, car mechanics, shysters and con artists to warrant the Jungle Image. Likewise, the Jungle Image holds for getting jobs and promotions. Back-stabbing, politicing, preferred credentials — it is hard to get attention, and the difficulty is precisely because of competition.

And yet the Jungle Image breaks down.

> Item. In business where the Jungle Image is derived and most popular competition of the jungle is not really at stake. In the largest business sector, small business arena, the trouble signs given by a veteran banker to a group of loan officers listed these problems, not one of which had to do with competition. The business was headed for trouble if there was: selling collateral without bank permission, no financial statement, to life insurance on owner, buying an expensive car for owner immediately after receiving a loan. (Wall Street Journal).

> Item. Competition prevails among those who are suited for it, for example car makers. And yet, competition is limited and bounded by cooperation: the car dealer mutual associations. The same is true for appliance dealers, real estate businesses.

> Item. The most productive worker (who is also the most attractive) is not the competitive back-stabber but the one who can cooperate. The person usually most valuable to and sought after by a company is the person who can work with people and draw out their talent and resources.

Healthy Competition. Because competition is universal and a fact of life, there are some guidelines which are needed as to come out of this distress better and stronger. First, be sure you have reached a level where you are strong enough to compete. This is the problem, by the way, for advocating competition too early for youths. In games, children need to be involved to find out what they can *do* — not to win. Youngsters too often come away from competitive games with broken spirts because competition was foisted upon them *before they* *are suited.* People become suited first by going through a phase of self-evaluation and self-discovery of their abilities and talents. Likewise for adults, before we compete we must learn what we can do, what our basic abilities are. Then, once we have developed those basic abilities in non-competitive moments, we will be *suited*, or equipped, to compete.

Picture competition as being healthy only on the Second Plateau.

> ***Plateau One:*** period of self-discovery and intitial development, until one's talents are sufficient in strength or reliability. This is "Try-out Time." The youth tries out his ability to throw, jump, discuss, bargain and so forth. The adult tries out his skill in math, selling, problem solving. He or she *re-hearses*. Re-hearsal is a necessary preparation for distress of competition.

> ***Plateau Two:*** The person is ready for the distress of competition because they have readied themselves for it: have identified their abilities, talents. Now they are suited to compare themselves more vigorously with others. At this stage of comparison (competition) the person will profit, will grow, and come out of it better — even if they lose the competition.

The problem with the competitive attitude is that it is urged too soon, before a person reaches "plateau two" and while one is at "plateau one." Because many persons are urged to compete before they know their abilities, they fail. They are either overwhelmed and stop trying: or, they get so anxious that they make mistakes and fail; or, they seek an escape such as not trying — thus no one can blame them even though they've "copped out." Or, they may seek to blame others: they pull the scapegoating act, that "It's not my fault but the other person who's to blame," or they may attempt to "win" by dishonest means of cheating or lying.

This is what misguided competitive people lead themselves and others (particularly their children) to do: make all sorts of ill-advised coping attempts:

   *Apathy
   *Escapes
   *Avoidances

Competitive persons teach children to try to "win" before their time, and before they know their abilities. The same competitive persons then are surprised when the youths are unmotivated, dishonest, failure prone, uninterested, and accusing of others. Producing a poor loser is the natural result of ill-timed emphasis upon competition.

Short Order Solution

Steps to take for Competition Distress

The most important steps for you will be (1) making decisions on your attitude toward Competition with its bearing toward your self-worth, (2) getting a firmer idea of your self worth coming from inner sources of being worthile, and (3) getting control of your life and time.

1) GET IT OUT. Talk with a good listener about some of the following attitudes.

— Proverbs like, "It's a jungle out there." Identify when in the last week or month your successes were more determined by competition rather than cooperation, and vice-versa. See if you would not have done better if you were able to cooperate with someone, using one another as resources.

— Complete this sentence: "One thing I know about competition: _____"

(For example, "I always find competition more attractive in a colleague than cooperation.") Do you find that it stands up to evidence of actual experience? Or is it only a half-truth, like the Jungle Image?

— You may say "I work best under pressure and competition." Do not be too sure. Discuss with your listener these questions (suggested by Alan Laiken):

(1) You may work hard under pressure, but do you work well? What evidence do you have for working well?

(2) Do you spend more time, because of confusion and lack of organization, by waiting to work under the deadline?

(3) Do you find it takes an emotional toll? Are there any of the clues of physical distress showing up in you?

(4) Do you behave badly to others when under pressure?

(5) Do you really enjoy or prefer working under pressure?

(6) Do you notice more the cost of fatigue after working under pressure?

2) GET A HANDLE. Your distress probably comes from self imposed expectations, which are self defeating. You have a distress with a structure (explained in Chapter Five) of Conflict: you are pulled between opposing forces. That is,

*On the one hand you want to do an excellent job, better than anyone else; you want to "beat them" and be a winner at all things.

*On the other hand, you always find someone who is a threat to you, seems to be better. And, you also find you alienate the people you need as resources. And, you know too that cooperation is probably more helpful in day-to-day activities than competition.

Conflict #2 best describes your distress. You have to make up your mind. That is, you need to set some priorities.

3) GET RID OF RIGIDITY. For you this means the rigidness which comes from high goals and perfectionism. Read the essay on "perfectionism" in Overload Distress. You also have rigid ideas of your self-worth coming from his misguided competition. Re-read the essay on "competition." Above all, take some active relaxaton exercises, given in Chapter Two.

4) SHORE UP YOUR STRENGTHS AND RESOURCES. Assess the arena where you are on Plateau One: unclear about your abilities, undeveloped in skills and opinions. Do NOT compete in situations here. For example:

— Computers
— Financial Figures
— Political Ideas

Identify where you are on Plateau Two: you see you have already achieved skills, training, abilities, in these areas. This is where you CAN compete.

5) ACTION PLANS

*Knowing your own strengths, play according to your own rules, not theirs.

*Set reasonable goals.

*If you are competitive, you probably need to acquire some more cooperative skills.

*Identify more closely what *you* want, and take steps on how to get control of your life and time, so as to feel good about your own self-image. Alan Laiken's excellent book, *How To Get Control of Your Life And Time* will help you to:

    a) Identify what is important to you in life.
    b) Translate your goals into action.
    c) Go through the Control-Of-Life.

*If you have evidence of a cardiac conditon, you will profit further by reading, such as the book, *Type A, Behavior and Your Heart,* by Friedman and Rosenman.

    d) Look again closely at your attitude to enhance yourself by comparing yourself constantly with others. Consider the following essay on the "Trouble With Comparing," and how it leads you to be in constant inner turmoil by an exaggerated emphasis on competition.

THE TROUBLE WITH COMPARING

We most likely cannot remember when we first compared ourself to others, but it was early in our life. "His toy isn't as good as mine... You cannot run as fast as I can... Am I better than so and so, Mom?" All such early comparisons find their type in the long-standing, "My dad can lick your dad!" And that was when we first got into trouble with comparisons — from our dad!

Through life we continue to compare ourselves without a rating system to ourself. Are we more than "they" or less?

More talented or less? More money in the bank, more sociable, more attractive — or less?

One thing is clear about this urge to compare: we did not get it in school. We went there with it. *We seem to start our conscious life with this urge to compare ourselves.* It sometimes leads us into problems. I strongly suspect we can use it to our advantage more than we do now.

If we did not rate ourselves, we would never know Self or our worth. The eye cannot see itself by reflection in a mirror; nor can we know ourselves except in the reflection which rebounds from others. At least, this is the beginning of self-knowledge.

What we need above all is to appreciate ourselves for what we really are. Our uniqueness, talents, ability, and all our strengths: these must be known and clear to us at the start of the good coping and healthy, satisfied living.

At the same time, when we are old enough to compare ourselves we are old enough to have a peril. Rating self with another brings a danger: If we at times become discouraged, envious, angry, conceited or ruthless, the explanation quite often can be found in the fact that, here again, we have compared ourselves to others. We still get into trouble with comparisons. There is both good news and bad news in our urge to compare. Suppose we look at both.

Benefits of comparing ourselves. Thanks to a very well founded psychological theory, the Social Comparison Theory first stated by Leon Festinger, we know these benefits of comparing ourselves.

>*We seem to be born with the tendency to know ourselves.
>
>*We want to know ourselves in three angles: our abilities, our opinions, and our feelings.
>
>*When there is no objective standard against which to rate these abilities, opinions and feelings, then we naturally seek other people and compare ourselves with them.
>
>*By adulthood, most abilities and opinions and feelings are only able to be known by comparing ourselves with others.

Perils of Comparing Ourselves. On the other hand, there are decidedly high risks to ourselves and our social relationships in this urge to compare.

Item: *It can lead us to continually feel the need to belittle others so as to enlarge ourselves. This is something which gets to be a stronger tendency the less we actually think of ourselves. It is like a "warp" in our personality. Which takes on more of a bent the less we think of ourselves. Harry Stack Sullivan said this peril is so great for some inadequate persons that they end up with the working attitude: "If I am a molehill, there will be no mountains." The person cuts everyone down to their own size.

Item: *When this urge to compare then takes tne form of winning and belittling, the person destroys in their own minds anyone to imitate. They destroy any chance for heroes — which is self-defeating.

Item: *Probably most destructive, however, is the risk upon the person themselves while comparing: they tend to underestimate their own worth and capability.

Item: *In comparing, we make our measure to be what we *observe* in others. How much they work, what they have in awards, what they gain by way of conspicuous standards. This is unfair to them: because we do not know their inner aims, desires; nor do we know their barriers, sicknesses, pressures. It's also unfair to us because our own desires and interests are compared to their conspicuous achievements, and ours are not the same as theirs.

Item: *The idea we get from comparing and competing with others is not often the most highly prized by those persons who mean the most to us. We are interesting but in ways different than we often thing. Most often we are valued for reasons quite contrary

I'm Doing My Best ... But It Isn't Enough

to what we think to be our worth. What makes others care for us frequently is not our strength but our admitted weakness. We are none of us terribly interesting on a pedestal. Friends see through it all; we may boast but they see the part of us which begs.

Once you see these perils of constantly comparing yourself, of constantly being "hooked into" competing with others to preseve your self-worth or to enhance, you'll begin to doubt this attitude. You will begin to want to temper your need to compare and compete in so many aspects of your life. And you will begin to know how right Konrad Lorenz was when it said, "Competition is a much greater evil in human life than aggression will ever be." He was given the Nobel Peace Prize for research leading to that conclusion. By coming to the same conclusion, you will gain for yourself a noble peace of mind.

Chapter Nine

Dilemmas Needing Your Initiative

Your action plans for your own dilemmas take differing paths. You have to tailor your strategy to your differing problems. Some solutions require a bold approach from you, while others require a very different approach. To make this point I would like to suggest what is often called the KISS method: KEEP IT SIMPLE, STUPID. I would like you to return to an earlier time when life was simpler and a man could write the following rhyme to put perspective on dealing with life's problems:

> For all your days prepare
>   And meet them ever alike;
> When you are an anvil, bear —
>   And when you are a hammer, strike. (Edwin Markem)

In this quaint ditty we have a tremendously important blueprint for selecting differing action plans. The trick is to know when you are anvil and when you are a hammer.

Most modern dilemmas do not permit such a simple two-sided direction to solutions. Still, you will profit by getting clear in your mind the differing paths you might attempt. There are distresses which are mainly resolved by your taking the initiative. This chapter is precisely about such difficulties and how to take that initiative, in conflicts with people particularly. At the outset of discussing these dilemmas, however, I must recall that you and others will often face dilemmas *where the ability to sustain is more important than to take the initiative*.

In the next chapter we will discuss those distresses where a person's solutions will be to "bear," to be an anvil in some fashion. Here we are going to be discussing the modified "hammer" approaches. By these I mean those dilemmas when we are going to come up with a solution by some form of active approach, some initiative which firmly but civilly confronts a difficulty. So "hammer" may cease to be a helpful word but the idea is the same: to actively expend efforts.

Initiative is the solution for various dilemmas such as the following:

* Conflicts between people
* Communication conflicts
* Inner distress of shyness
* Distress of feeling guilty about hurting feelings of others
* Boredom — surprisingly!

We Americans are doubtlessly more prepared for the hammer-like solutions. The American mood is to be aggressive. Our customs in solving problems as a nation has been, at various times, to slash through a forest, strike out at a frontier, spearhead business and mobilize machines. These solutions become institutionalized and then are passed on to us in our individual lives. Our brand of coping with conflicts and frustrations is to be more aggressive — in the vein of being a hammer.

Confronting By Healthy Attack

A major way of coping with problems is by direct action. Let us look at some examples of some stresses handled by such directness.

> Ralph's job threat centers around a threat of being laid off. He was transferred from being a catalog sales clerk to the shipping dock, without explanation. He found this stressful not because of being unmotivated to work but because he had had a nine year history of deteriorating nerves in his wrist and was unable to life heavy boxes; he needed surgery on his wrist. When he informed the personnel office of his handicap, he was told his services were no longer needed with the company.

Gene was in a family stress where the threat of taking care of three generations of his family became too overwhelming. He was the adoptive single parent of two boys, working full time and going to school part-time. At one point, his parents invited themselves to live with Gene; his father had just had neurosurgery, had been in a coma for a month with the result that his mother required hospitalization with a cardiac condition. Gene's parents therefore were in a weakened condition upon moving in with him. Gene had to do all the cooking and housekeeping, in addition to work, study and parenting his children.

Ida is in a job stress with a supervisor who continually gives her reports and projects beyond what she is able to do, the other staff at her level doing little. She is called upon to give inservice training. Her personal life suffers because she takes home with her all the worries of unfinished tasks. As a result her sexual life with her husband suffers because she cannot relax enough at home.

Judith faced stress in the form of a threat during her pregnancy. She was in her eighth month and in a new city when she went to see (Army appointed an obstetrician. To Judith and her husband, the physician made this immediate statement in the form of a self-authorized decision: "Since this is your fourth child, after this delivery we will do a tubal ligation."

Joyce feared the stress of being in the middle of her college degree program, returning after raising a family, when her husband was transferred to a foreign country which would offer her no prospects for continuing her education. She felt cheated out of the chance to get her degree and pursue her own career as a teacher. She wanted to tell her husband she did not want to go with him to his foreign assignment, but she also felt a duty to go with him anywhere to keep the family together. The stress was a threat — of how he would react, and it hung on for two months.

TAKING ACTION AGAINST OUR STRESSES

Having cleared up that there are some stresses which call for an attacking approach on our part and other stresses which will call for a more sustaining stance as we work problems through, we can now begin to map our strategy for both.

We recall from Chapter Five that there are these actions open to us.

1) First, for whatever our stress, we take actions to *strengthen* ourselves.

2) Then we will decide if we can take any *direct actions* to attack the stress problem. But we must be careful to see the difference between direct actions which are appropriate and those which are of an out-of-control rage. So, direct actions can be "healthy" confrontations or "unhealthy" outbursts.

3) Some actions we can take to *avoid problems*, and these too can be healthy or unhealthy. Healthy avoidances are temporary reliefs, strategic withdrawals; unhealthy avoidances are escapisms used repeatedly without returning to handle the problem. The unhealthy avoidances are the dead-ends; healthy avoidances are more like temporary detours.

4) Finally, we can decide to take *no action*, and this strategy also may be a healthy suspending of activity while restrenghtening ourselves or searching for better solutions; or it can be apathy, an inertia while wanting to be "rescued" or thinking the problem will go away. The first inaction is healthy, the second is quite self-defeating.

Let us recall our program of stress which we have outlined all along 1) First, we handle stress by getting out, by talking to a helpful listener. 2) Then we get a handle on the problem, by seeing whether the problem is one of a Conflict or a Frustration. 3) We then rid ourselves of rigidity. 4) With step four, we strengthen ourselves — which is actually a way to start our coping actions.

First Action of Coping

Throughout these pages we have listed various ways of strenghtening ourselves.

The aim of this first direction action is to soften, if not do away with, that which is a threat to us. The first way in general is to *assess our resources*. As we saw in Chapter Seven, these include resources of three kinds: a) resources within ourselves; b) the resources in other people who are close to us, friends and family; and c) resources in our community.

Exactly how we strengthen ourselves depends on our own particular stress; that is, what will be a strong point or "muscle" need for our particular problem. For example, we strengthen ourselves by building storm shelters if tornadoes are our threat; by developing social skills if our threat is the fear of being lonely or rejected; by building up our savings account or credit rating when fearing financial threats, by building our self-reliance when our threat is disapproval by others. And so on.

Three Forms of Attack

In each of these we have a stress which is attackable, to which we can take a "hammer" approach in the sense we spoke of earlier. There are two ways we can attack such a stress: by either an adaptive coping of confronting the problem or mainly with an emotional outburst which is out of control. In brief, we can hammer or attack directly with trained feeling or with outright rages; either constructive or destructive.

So this alternative can be, if in rage, destructive. This is the direct action strategy which most people immediately think of and many have in their emergency set of skills, to strike out hostility, aggressively, perhaps with vengeance. It is the option chosen by people who think first of suing, slugging, slashing; it is the strategy at work in many divorce settlements, in those given to child abuse to control their child, or in the retaliating of setting fire to a place which has fired a person from a job.

In the examples just given, this alternative would lead Ralph to a fistfight with his supervisor, would impel Gene to belittle his parents as he disclaims responsibility for them, Ida to get so furious with her boss that in her anger she would say explosive things which would leave them forever at odds, Judith would walk from her physician in a tantrum and Joyce would call her husband names.

Equally possible, if this approach is not used right, the people would walk away from their stress situation, but still have their hurt feelings and indeed the same rage, but it would be pent up. They hold back their feelings, say nothing. Yet, somehow the anger turns inside themselves and they get headaches, muscle tension, and an increased set of physical ailments (like Fact Two, described in Chapter Four). The anger and direction action is there, only directed inwardly against themselves.

Holding our anger in, directing it against ourself is not helpful. So too, attacking with anger full out does not appear to be adaptive. Indeed the coping with rage is in the main a primitive means of coping. Experience indicates that it may indeed restore some semblance of balance, though not in a satisfactory way. For one thing, the feelings live on within us even when they have been expressed hostilely; the feelings we have are of satisfaction which are paired with hostility, which can eat at us and just may make us more hostile in other stress. Handling a stress with rage is a sure way to come out of the stress worse than we went into it. With rage we are deteriorated, indeed *weakened for future stresses.*

Assertiveness, on the other hand, is a set of skills for this direction action option: to face squarely and confront the threat as best we can. The best direct action plan is *Confrontation.* It is the direct handling of a problem, and found to be the most helpful or adaptive of all.

In brief, there are three ways to handle conflicts and stresses with people. They are summarized nicely by Alberti and Emmons in *Your Perfect Right:*

NON-ASSERTIVE BEHAVIOR	AGGRESSIVE BEHAVIOR	ASSERTIVE BEHAVIOR
As Actor	As Actor	As Actor
Self-denying	Self-enhancing at expense of another	Self-enhancing
Inhibited	Expressive	Expressive
Hurt, anxious	Depreciates others	Feels good about self
Allows others to choose for him	Chooses for others	Chooses for self
Does not achieve desired goal	Achieves desired goal by hurting others	May achieve desired goal
As Acted Upon	As Acted Upon	As Acted Upon
Guilty or angry	Self-denying	Self-enhancing
Depreciates actor	Hurt, defensive humiliated	Expressive
Achieves desired goal at actor's expense	Does not achieve desired goal	May achieve desired goal

Appropriate assertiveness is a way of exercising personal *strength*. And from the exercise comes the experience of strength. Assertiveness enables us to experience strength in a variety of situations, meeting a variety of needs.

In assertiveness we become practiced to express our own appropriate needs and rights in such a way as to take into account the needs and rights of others. It practices us to express our feelings, to compliment others, to state our convictions, to admit to our positive values. This trained anger will also permit us, with benefits to ourselves, to be rid of additions and quirks ruining our own lives, preventing the fulfillment of loyalties, and achieving our intimacies.

In brief, for those stresses which can be attacked or assaulted, there is no better skill than that of assertiveness. Not all stresses can be attacked, but for those that can be, assertiveness is the key. We may have to blend it with other actions (to be discussed shortly). We may have to blend our assertiveness with healthy delays or constructive inaction, or with strategic and temporary retreats. But when they are in the right mixture, assertiveness will provide the best spearhead of our attacking certain stresses. In other words, assertiveness as a skill is the linchpin of directly confronting many stresses.

COPING WITH STRESSES WHICH CAN BE ATTACKED

What all the above stresses have in common is Anger. Anger-stresses are somehow among the most frequent kinds of stresses today. We live so close together, have so many personal conflicts, go at such a demanding pace, and have such multiple demands. The threat of Anger-stress is a thoroughly modern stress.

Anger-stresses are among the most changeable, potentially, but they are also among the most volatile. While the above are attackable stresses, they are also laden with explosiveness and capable, if handled incorrectly, of bringing additional threats with each blundering coping. For example, Richard can be blackballed with a bad work record and Joyce's marriage might develop a gap of misunderstanding which becomes a chasm.

Anger-stresses, to be coped with adaptively, need to be first dealt with mentally: our *attitudes* toward anger itself.

1. Attitudes to Re-Shape

Mental stretch of the road in anger-stresses. On the positive side, our anger in these stresses should be seen for its adaptive value: it is a need for justice experienced; it is also a demand that some change or adjustment is in order.

Anger ought to be more prized. I am not so much suggesting that we ought to have an Annual Anger Week as we have Memorial Day, but I am suggesting we value it long enough to see that anger is one of our main tools for experiencing *strength*.

Many things will never get done unless we get angry. In this sense, many people get both too little and too much — they are usually the same people. On the one hand, they are angry too little at their own procrastination, neglect, self-pity, self-hurting behaviors such as over-eating, smoking, drinking; they are particularly too little angry at their self-defeating illusions by letting them go on and on. They could use anger adaptively by attacking anything within themselves that prevents them from being the person they would like to be, realistically.

The same people, on the other hand, are also likely to be angry too much: at the insensitivity of a spouse or work partner, at negligence and irresponsibility of *others*, most of all at "unfairness." Griping, gossiping, "goldbricking," mimicking all patterns of indirect anger, arising because a person is not directly expressing his anger.

The first problem with anger is when its aim is wrong: directed toward what we have no control over, or not expect to exercise control over. Healthy anger is directed in an attack over which we have control but is presently controlled and is ruining our life: procrastination, delusions of self-pity and grandeur and the like. This directed anger can provide us the control over our life which will revitalize us. Deliberate, controlled assertion is the best policy. The healthy coper is of necessity an angry person — with an accurate aim.

Coping anger takes the form of a protest for a just cause, a fair share, a square deal, reversing not just a misfortune but a misfortune which is seen as an injury.

The second shortcoming of anger is its blind impulsiveness. People are primed for aggressiveness. The trouble is that they have taken the first, mental stretch of the road down one of the deadends: they get lost in one of their unreal fantasies. Anger is easily able to be duped. Take for example what happens with the word, "Mine." We start by saying "my pencil — perfectly legitimate." I own the pencil, can do with it whatever I wish. But then the phrase becomes "My traffic lane, my company, my spouse, my child" — and we have extended the same (fantasied) rights of ownership to these people and situations as we did to our pencil. We act with the same authority and imperiousness, but we have overstepped our rights and exaggerated our claims.

The more claims a person has, the more easily he or she can be offended and therefore live a lifestyle of anger, injustice. If a person lets the imagination make up a long list of "claims" there is no end to their stress of being hurt or angry.

Anger which has become rage is a coping which has taken the wrong turn down the mental stretch of the road. Indeed the problem with anger is illustrated in the testy, rageful driver: "That other guy is driving in MY lane, took MY spot!!" The anger of a raged driver has hurts in the driver's seat.

2. Actions To Take

The action stretch of the road. When we, like Richard or Gene or Ida, face an Injustice stress there are basically only three ways to go, three paths to take: we can let our anger go full out and aggressively assault the person involved; or we can hold our anger in, seethe and simmer but meekly submit; or, we can mobilize our anger into an adaptive coping and *assert* ourselves.

Assertiveness is talked about much today. It is well it should receive so much attention for it is an eminent skill for coping with Injustice Stresses so frequent in today's living. There are assertiveness training opportunities everywhere. The same training is invariably a major focus in any book or article dealing with stress.

I agree that assertiveness training is most helpful. At the same time, I see reason for those who say, "Enough already; no more assertivness training," or who claim it does not solve all problems, it is not a panacea.

After all, assertiveness training *is* an SOS response — a short order solution. Until we see it in its legitimate perspective, and place it within our lifestyle, it will disappoint us. Not all stresses can be handled by assertiveness. And those which are appropriate to assertiveness training require a bit more tailoring of the skill than is frequently done. As anything, assertivenesss training has become a fad and a fad fades when it is inflated to do what was never intended or designed for.

In brief, assertiveness refers to any socially acceptable expression of personal rights and feelings, according to its originators Wolfe and Lazarus. Assertiveness is the action of declaring about oneself, "This is who I am and what I think and feel." It requires an honest, relatively straightforward expression of feelings; of anger, yes, but also of affection and pride, as well as of feelings of dissatisfaction, disappointment or resentment.

But above all, assertiveness is appropriate: an expression of one's self which is in order and called for. We have a *right*, real not fantasized, and we give a reasonable expression to that right; right for redress, acknowledgement.

When we have Injustice Stresses, such as those mentioned earlier, assertiveness is the adaptive coping of choice. Assertive behavior is our choosing to act as to promote our own interest, to stand up for ourselves without undue anxiety, to express our rights *without denying the rights of others*. Our assertiveness is reasonable, in order and appropriate when that last condition is fulfilled — "without denying the (real) rights of others."

A list of various kinds of assertiveness responses have been indicated by Alberti and Emmons:

NINE TYPES OF ASSERTIVE RESPONSES

1. *Assertive talk.* Do not let others take advantage of you. Demand your rights. Insist upon being treated with fairness and justice. Examples: "I was here first," "I'd like more coffee, please," "Excuse me, but I have another appointment," "Please turn down the radio," "This place is a pigsty," "You have kept me waiting here for half an hour," "This steak is well-done and I ordered it medium-rare."

2. *Feeling talk.* Express your likes and dislikes spontaneously. Be open and frank about your feelings. Do not bottle up emotions. Answer questions honestly. Examples: "What a marvelous shirt!" "I am so sick of that man," "How great you look!" "I hate this cold,: "I'm tired as hell," "Since you ask, I much prefer you in another type of outfit."

3. *Greeting talk.* Be outgoing and friendly with people whom you would like to know better. Do not avoid people because of shyness, because you do not know what to say. Smile brightly at people. Look and sound pleased to see them. Examples: "Hi, how are you?" "Hello, I haven't

seen you in months." "What are you doing with yourself these days?" "How do you like working at...?" "Taking any good courses?" "What's been happening with so and so?"

4. *Disagreeing passively and actively.* When you disagree with someone, do not feign agreement for the sake of "keeping the peace" by smiling, nodding or paying close attention. Change the topic. Look away. Disagree actively and emotionally when you are sure of your ground.

5. *Asking why.* When you are asked to do something that does not sound reasonable or enjoyably by a person in power or authority, ask why you should do it. You are an adult and should not accept authority alone. Insist upon explanations from teachers, relatives and other authority figures that are convincing. Have it understood that you will live up to voluntary commitments and be open to reasonable suggestions, but that you are not to be ordered about at anyone's whim.

6. *Talking about oneself.* When you have done something worthwhile or interesting, let others know how you feel about things. Relate your experiences. Do not monopolize conversations, but do not be afraid to bring them around to yourself when it is appropriate.

7. *Agreeing with compliments.* Do not depreciate yourself or become flustered when someone compliments you with sincerity. At the very least, offer an equally sincere "Thank you," Or reward the complimenter by saying, "That's an awfully nice thing to say. I appreciate it." In other words, reward rather than punish others for complimenting you. When appropriate, extend compliments. For example if someone says, "What a beautiful sweater," respond, "Isn't it a lovely color? I had a hard time finding it."

8. *Avoiding trying to justify opinions.* Be reasonable in discussions, but when someone goes out of his way to dominate a social interaction by taking issue with any comment you offer, say something like, "Are you always

so disagreeable?" or "I have no time to waste arguing with you," or "You seem to have a great deal invested in being right regardless of what you say, don't you?"

9. ***Looking people in the eye.*** Do not avoid the gaze of others. When you argue, express an opinion, or greet a person, look him directly in the eye.

The essence of assertiveness if that of being a direct action which is productive. The key idea about being assertive is to deliberately express what one's perceived rights are, what one's feelings are within a context of *respecting the rights and feelings of others*.

In concrete situations, like work situations similar to those of Ralph and Ida, you can see how the three ways of direct taking action differ.

WORKING LATE

You and your spouse have an evening engagement which has been planned for several weeks. Today is the date and you plan to leave immediately after work. During the day, however, your supervisor indicates that he would like to stay late this evening to work on a special assignment.

Alternative Responses:

(a) You say nothing about your important plans and simply agree to stay until the work is finished.

(b) In a nervous, abrupt voice you say "No, I will not work late tonight." Then you criticize the boss for not planning the work schedule better. You then turn back to work you were doing.

(c) Talking to the supervisor in a firm, but pleasant voice, you tell of your important plans and say you will not be able to stay this evening to work on the special assignment.

JOB ERROR

You have made a mistake on some aspect of your job. Your supervisor discovers it and is letting you know rather harshly that you should not have been so careless. Alternative Responses:

(a) Overapologizing, you say you are sorry, you were stupid, how silly of you, you'll never let it happen again.
(b) You bristle up and say that he has no business whatsoever criticizing your work. You tell him to leave you alone and not bother you in the future because you are capable of handling your own work.
(c) You agree that you made the mistake, say you are sorry and will be more careful next time. You add that you feel he is being somewhat harsh and you see no need for that.

The point is, in being assertive: express your needs and rights while also respecting the other person. As a rule this will work out better if you start your statements with, "I" (e.g. "I am really frustrated and feel that I have a right to more advanced notice about such reports." "I am feeling unfairly treated by the change you are suggesting.") Starting with "I" lets the other person see that *you* are seeing a problem, and want to share what you see as a solution. On the other hand, good assertiveness does not *label* ("You're inconsiderate") nor imput motives ("You're always trying to get me.") These things lead to aggressive fights which escalate arguments.

Three Do's and Don'ts of Assertive Talk. Assertiveness clearly pertains to taking direct action when the stress is conflict with people. Thus, assertive talk is close to good constructive openness. And we might summarize three rules for constructive assertiveness, and three things to avoid so as to prevent our assertiveness from being seen as aggression — which then leads to rage and more intense conflicts.

DO'S OF ASSERTIVE OPENESS

(1) Describe your own feelings: "I like what you just said. "I feel blue." "I am irritated."
(2) Describe behaviors related to your feelings: "I'm annoyed when you interrupt me like that." "I feel hurt when you re-assign me to those jobs."

(3) Check outlooks. "I'm confused. Do I understand it right: you would like to have me take over that role, but you do not intend this to be a demotion for me?"

DON'TS: THE AGGRESSIVE RESPONSES

(1) Name-calling: labelling: "you're rude." "You're a phoney, inconsiderate, etc."
(2) Accusing of motives: "you always want to be top dog." "You keep trying to put me down."
(3) Commands and orders. "Don't do it this way." "Stop that."

IN THE CONCRETE SITUATION

Simply remember one word: "I." All the do's begin with "I." Likewise all the dont's begin with one word: "You" (are inconsiderate, want to be the center of attention, etc.) Make only "I" statements. Avoid "You" statements.

In conclusion, good assertiveness is the healthy way of directly attacking people problems. You do not always get what you want, but it is the best way to try and is the most helpful way of dealing with stresses which can be attacked where people are concerned.

Aggressiveness puts *trained anger* at our disposal. Anger can get "wild" at times. And there are three things you can do with a wild animal: cage it, unleash it as it is, or train it. If you cage it, the anger will eventually break out with more violence than you can handle; if you unleash it it will assault destructively; but if you train it, your anger can be one of the greatest strengths for stress you can have.

Eventually, every healthy coping strategy comes back to being some form of direct action, some form of confrontation.

Some things in life deserve our trained anger. Erich Fromm once said, "A man sits in front of a bad television program and does not know he is bored . . . If enough people become aware of their shared misery, they will probably effect changes. Anger may often be less sick than adjustment."

Probably people should come to the point in the old movie, "Network:" "I'm mad as hell and I'm not going to take it any more." If anger is aroused and used assertively, it can be adaptive. Trained anger can eliminate some threats; that failing, it can allow one to relieve self of the stress of pent up feelings and injured rights.

Chapter Ten

Toughing Out a Distress Which Will Not Vanish Nor Diminish

A VALIUM LIFE STYLE

The most frequently prescribed drug in the United States is valium. Its use and overuse is probably very significant. Valium represents a life style and changed values. According to a recent authority on drugs.

> The enormous use of valium and other anti-anxiety agents may be a consequence of a recent shift in cultural values. It may no longer be a virtue to "tough out" noxius emotions as in old days. Using chemicals for relief is currently an acceptable alternative for large segments of the population.
>
> (Cohen, 1981)

I strongly suspect that Cohen is correct. More and more people appear to believe that it is not necessary nor fair nor acceptable (let alone desirable) to tough out problems.

With such a change in life style, however, we may be making it harder to deal with stress and distress. We may be making it more difficult to solve certain dilemmas. This belief, that one should not or will not, tough out problems runs head to head with certain distresses. One kind of distress will not go away quickly. Other kinds of distress seem not to go away at all.

WHEN YOUR DISTRESS DOES NOT QUICKLY VANISH

In all of people's distresses and dilemmas there comes a point when one must recall one basic fact. This fact is

I'm Doing My Best... But It Isn't Enough

becoming less and less obvious today. Nevertheless, this one fact must be faced: *Stress and distress rarely go away quickly.* Rarely do they arise overnight; even more infrequently do they vanish suddenly.

In stress and distress we all live in a "time-zone." That is, we live in an experience which takes time to develop and also takes time to solve. I find people really begin to cope well when they take seriously the following:

> Put up in a place
> Where it's easy to see
> The cryptic admonishment:
> > T.T.T.
>
> When you feel how depressingly
> Slowly you climb,
> It's well to remember that
> > THINGS TAKE TIME.

You've heard of erogenous zones, "erroneous zones," sound zones, and time zones. You need to take the time zones particularly seriously in distress and stress — the TTT zones, as it were.

In a day of rapid travel, immediate computer turn-over, instant communication, push-button responses in the machines all around us, we need to recall our own Time Zones. You and I and all of us need this reminder. We are so surrounded by the "instant" reactions that we tend to forget that not everything will react instantly.

We are surrounded by quick and easy shopping, fast-food restaurants, five-step recipes on dieting; we are engulfed with machines which hurry your pace in communication, information gathering, and productiveness. Our technology has everywhere increased the speed of our lives. That speed in most areas will only increase. We might therefore be deceived when we try to handle personal, human problems.

Particularly dangerous to coping with distress are pills: they offer such immediate relief and we mistake them for a solution. The valiums, barbiturates, amphetamines and anti-depressants — they all seem to suggest a better life through instant chemistry. Still, the assuaging effects are mainly a mask. Real solutions, long-term solutions, are not quickly produced. Things take time, particularly stress and distress. The valium life style may not be a style for solutions.

In distress people are involved and people do not function like a communication switchboard or a computer. Human feelings do not arise and evaporate like computer data, or respond to some secret "off" button. Human decision making is not like a computer program, as we saw in Chapter Five.

Stress and distress put us in a totally new arena. Much of the new inventive technology will not apply to stress coping. We have to step back from a frenzied pace and search for quickie solutions.

STRESS TURNED TO DISTRESS
WHICH WILL NOT GO AWAY

Consider the circumstance of Helen.

> Helen experienced the stress of learning at age forty she had given birth to a baby with Down's Syndrome, meaning the child was severely retarded. Helen felt guilty because she somehow thought she was responsible for the defect. She experienced anger at the doctor for not telling her of possible complications in a birth at her age. But mostly she feels fatigued and pessimistic at the prospects that she can do so little for the child. At times she wishes either she or the child would die. She wanted to place the child in some care agency, but this was met with anger from her two other daughters and her husband.

Helen's plight is a clear reminder that some stresses simply do not go away or cannot be "assaulted."

Every stress of illness or handicap is a reminder that some stresses require staying-power, the ability to sustain. The image of an anvil is quite vivid. An anvil is a heavy piece of metal on which metal is shaped. *An anvil can take a pounding and not fall apart.* This is what is needed for some stresses.

So, do not believe a person who says there are quick and easy solutions to all stresses, that all you have to do is find the right way to attack the problem. Some stresses are not of that kind. You know this of course, but you need to be very conscious of it when mapping strategies.

Yes, there are stresses which can be attacked. We have talked of them in the past two chapters. Now we must admit there are others which are totally different, like illnesses, personality defects, financial problems from the economy (through no fault of our own) and so on. There are other stresses, turned distress, which demand we "bear up" — as anvils.

Probably those distresses which put a person most to the test of being able to bear up are those of *lacks*. If we lack certain important conditions, we are apt to experience distresses which seem not to go away. For example,

*Lack of health
*Lack of finances
*Lack of training
*Lack of companionship and intimacy
*Lack of family harmony, cooperation and closeness
*Lack of interest or challenge at work
*Lack of employment

And on and on and on. It is the lacks which we cannot assault that seem to require the most of us and seem the most impossible to bear up under.

Life's hardest demand is that we put-up-with.

(People are told never to end a sentence with a preposition. But I fancy that it's for amateurs. The English language, reflecting life, is not so finely tailored. As Winston Churchill once replied for being chided about prepositions: "This is the sort of English up with which I shall not put.")

Life's dilemmas and distresses push us to the extreme on occasion and make us put-up-with. And so we must speak. We have all sorts of things we must put-up-with. Intrusions into our privacy, humongous organizations, unrelenting weather of cold and drought and flooding, stupidly erroneous computers, crowded streets and highways, not to mention inconsiderate persons. In brief, life is for those who will, on occasion, put-up-with. And some distressing dilemmas provide the sternest occasions of all.

You would never mistake a missile for a pillar. For the same reason, never mistake your capacity to assert control for another capacity, to sustain. You will need to sustain what cannot be changed, at least quickly or easily.

One mark of a person adapting well to life and solving dilemmas is that he or she can wait for what they want when this is necessary and unavoidable. The effective coper can do what we have been discussing in these pages: put their dilemma in a time-zone, show the capacity to bear with some unavoidable obstacles, put up with some difficulties. All of this I will now summarize as STAYING-POWER. If your distressful dilemma will not go away, or seems not to be diminishing at all, then you will need the tools for staying power.

TOOLS FOR STAYING-POWER

The staying-power which will be necessary for you at times requires more than the saying, "hang in there," "tough it out," "bear with it," or other such simplistic bromides. Staying-power requires that you equip yourself in a very special way with special tools.

The tools which you need are ones with which you are already familiar if you have read all of the chapters to this point. In particular, it is by knowing "the three vulnerabilities" discussed in Chapter Seven that you will be able to see yourself through your most difficult dilemmas. These three vulnerabilities expose your greatest capacities in going through the really difficult dilemmas. The tools you will need are: (1) to know your own needs, and perhaps to change them; (2) to know your own resources and to use them; (3) to be aware of your own attitudes, and to use them when they are helpful and disgard them when they are self-defeating.

TOOL ONE: KNOW YOUR NEEDS, YOU MAY WANT TO CHANGE THEM

In Chapter Seven we spoke of three vulnerabilities to different forms of stress and distress. These vulnerabilities enabled you to identify which forms of distress you are most suspectible to.

Your own needs will in large part determine in which dilemma you will find most difficult to show staying power. It is

I'm Doing My Best . . . But It Isn't Enough

your needs which make your distress so unique to you. Because a need is precisely where the pain is in a distressing dilemma, and because needs are so personal, it is said that stress and distress are somehow "in the eye of the beholder." You remember from Chapter Seven that differing needs predispose differing persons to such stresses and distresses as: overload, competition, burnout, boredom, loneliness and to such capabilities as the ability to assert oneself.

Now let us return to the first step in using this tool, your needs: the step of assessing your needs. I will begin by presenting you with an image to help you live with the awareness of your needs and their meaning to your distress. Then I'll suggest some implications for particular distresses requiring staying power with your own needs. I want to give you a self-image — in stripes.

SHOWING YOUR STRIPES IN DISTRESS

To appreciate the role of needs in stress, we must be vividly aware of two facts: we bring a lot of needs to each situation and they vary in strength. To put this vividly in your mind's eye, I suggest seeing yourself in stripes — "showing your stripes." Look now at Figure 10-1.

We each wear a striped shirt or skirt as we approach a situation which may become stressful. Imagine your stripes to be about four in number, all are red in color and each about one inch wide. The red stripes are separated by a line of color of your choice — gold, white, whatever. The special thing about your shirt is that each of the stripes ascends to a different height: the one on the far right may be up to your shoulder while on the far left it may ascend half way up your vest; the others are of varying heights. Any person you know has a similar striped shirt or skirt but with a significant difference: their stripes each extend upward to a different degree than anyone else's.

Everyone has a different pattern of stripe heights. The top of the stripe is its "ceiling." And so the point of this fancied apparel is that each stripe is a need which we bring to a stress situation. Each need has a ceiling, unique to ourselves. When the uppermost part of that need is reached, we are stressed. When only the lower part of that need is reached, we are

Figure 10-1

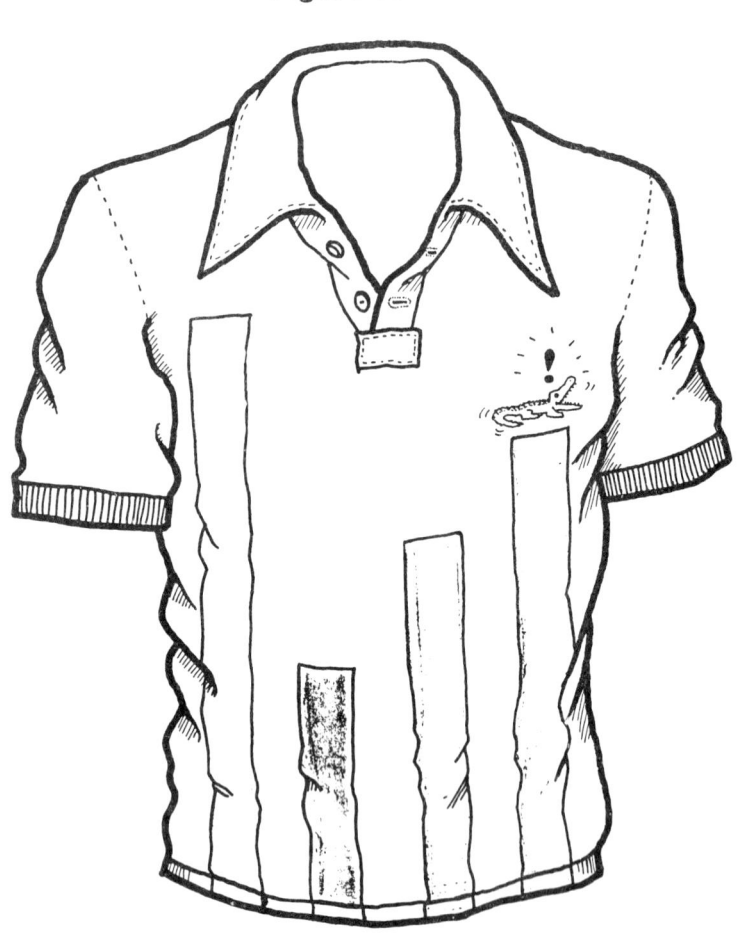

merely stimulated or challenged. A threat however is a stress when we have a high need which is in danger of not being met.

I think you can profit by assuming you take more needs than one into any situation. But you will confuse yourself if you think of more than three or four.

POINT ONE: YOUR NEEDS MAY BE FEW

The Fantasy of the striped shirt/skirt has several useful lessons. First of course is the fact that you can profit by seeing that you do take more needs than one into any situation, including stress. But you will confuse yourself if you think of more than three or four. While a large number of needs have been identified, you need not be concerned with them all. In fact, stress researcher Mechanic has said "there is some reason to belief that in many life endeavors too much self awareness or introspection retards successful coping efforts. Many successful copers tend to be rather insensitive to their own (inner) experiences and tend to orient themselves more to their outer environment than to their inner world."

There is a middle ground: some looking at our inner needs but not too much. We should have just enough to see the second lesson of the striped shirt fantasy: that is, you do not go into a stress "cold," as it were. You bring to every stress a pre-stress personality. This pre-stress personality is the source of both your strength and vulnerability when coping with stress. Before you are in a state of stress you are developing inner states, your needs. The striped shirt is a reminder you come dressed for stress, if you please, in your own way.

Figure 10-2

Maslow's Need Hierarchy

Listed below are five categories of needs identified by Abraham Maslow. They are arranged from low to high in terms of the extent to which they allow us to rise above a basic level of existence. Thus, physiological needs are considered lower-order needs, while self-actualization needs are of a higher order.

I. Physiological
Examples of Needs Included in Category:
Hunger
Thirst
Sex
Sleep
Rest
Exercise

II. Safety
Examples of Needs Included in Category:
Shelter
Protection from immediate or future danger to physical well-being
Protection from immediate or future threat to psychological or economic well-being.

III. Social
Examples of Needs Included in Category:
Love and affection
Friendship
Association with others
Affiliation

IV. Self-esteem
Examples of Needs Included in Category:
Self-confidence
Independence
Achievement
Competence
Knowledge
Status
Personal recognition
Respect
Influence over others

V. Self-actualization
Examples of Needs Included in Category:
Realizing one's potential
Self-development activities
Behaving creatively

Problem-centered orientation to life
Identifying with the problems of mankind
Acceptance of self and others

Abraham Maslow has compiled a very popular list of needs, as seen in Figure 10-2. For now it is enough to know that the needs most likely to show up in your stresses are basically quite few. However, they are of a special variety: your stress related needs are those which involve you as a person and, very often, other people. I have found that the following needs merit a close look by anyone preparing for a stress or distress:

*the need for achievement
*the need for sociability
*the need for intimacy
*the need for recognition
*the need for inner strength or personal power over one's life

POINT TWO: YOU CAN TEACH AN OLD DOG NEW TRICKS

So, the first important fact about showing your stripes is that your needs are few in number. The second key idea is that your needs can be changed — and it is *you* who can change them. That's the good news. You can lower or raise the "level" of your need as is called for in adjusting to your difficult dilemma.

The bad news is that you may create your own barrier to changing your need. You can refuse to think you can change. You can handicap your own change by the old bromide, "You can't teach an old dog new tricks. I'm just that way; I can't change."

Preparing for specially difficult dilemmas may begin with the acceptance that you *can change,* and maybe must change. You'll have to replace the "old dog" with the newer line, "He who is too old to learn was always too old to learn." Yes, you can change. How? By knowing the key ingredient of needs.

The Key Ingredient of Needs

Your needs are changeable because they are at their core simply *expectations,* which can be raised or lowered. Your need to achieve success is what you *expect* to have done, what you have planned or hoped for. Your need for approval and social acceptance is what you *expect* to receive from others. All personal and social needs — those causing most stresses — are like that, simply expectations. Needs are simply mental images of what we hope for. Needs are not hormones or muscular tissue or neurological networks which are fixed and sealed.

Because your need for achieving success may be high, it can be changed to help you cope with Overload Stress. If your need for competition is too high, it can be lowered to a more realistic level as you face the stress of impossible demands. If your need for social acceptance is too high, it can be lowered to face the threat of being rejected by others or passed over for a promotion.

The "old dog" you cannot teach has got to go if you are going to cope with upcoming stress. If your stress or distress is hanging on you may find you may need to change your expectations. Some of the solution may come from doing something within you. In many of the most difficult situations, the secret of life is *more in learning to like or accept what you do rather than doing what you like or would prefer.*

CHANGING NEEDS WHEN HANDICAPPED

One of the severest distresses come from a particular "lack:" that of physical health and well being. How could one know what needs are pressing on yourself here, so that you could better show staying power in this distress? As we mentioned in Chapter Seven, we can first identify the needs by assessing one's fears.

Every need has a corresponding fear, which is brought out by a particular stress. For example, a person with a strong need to achieve success has an equally deep fear of failure. A person with a strong need for sociability and approval has a deep fear of being left out of social gatherings and confidences of friends. The fears surface with the threats of stress. One woman told me she never realized how important her

I'm Doing My Best . . . But It Isn't Enough

need for intimacy was until she was stressed with the decision to separate from her husband.

Fear of Being Injured/Crippled. Consider another potential stress, that of the prospect of being crippled. What for *you* would be the most dire consequences of such a condition? What would *you* most fear? Again put a check beside any of the following actual statements made by persons who have received visible injuries.

"I FEAR:"
- __ People would consider my injury, not me as a person, as of prime importance.
- __ That the injury would devalue me as a person.
- __ That I would feel guilty for being a burden.
- __ I would be constantly torn between wanting independence while necessarily being dependent.
- __ I would be likely to wallow in self-pity and shrivel as a person.

You can see that the background of motives determines what is threatening, and stressful, to an injured person. The fears reveal strong needs for self-worth, for independence, control.

In sum, your needs and their fears are the most crucial vulnerability in preparing for your own stresses upcoming. Assess your needs well. Then you can begin to change the expectations in your needs. But the next two tools are terribly important to you. You must further go into your attitudes and, even more important, use a wide range of resources.

TOOL TWO: YOUR ATTITUDES

When you require staying-power, you will find that the second tool you need is to be aware of your attitudes. An attitude is very close to a mood which we have just discussed. In fact the two of them work very much as twin parts, or in tandem. They should be understood together in order to help you see yourself through a distress that seems not to go away. If you see them separately and together you will begin to understand some solutions which come in the third tool, your resources.

Needs come to conscious light in the forms of expectations, as I just said. Needs are very complicated. There are a wide variety of ways to categorize them. They can be seen from differing points of view, physiological as well as psychological. But for our purposes, you can think of them as coming down to *expectations which are rather temporary.* Attitudes, on the other hand, are more abiding beliefs. Our attitudes or beliefs regulate our optimism or pessimism of things to come.

Richard Lazarus, always so insightful about coping with stress and distress, clearly shows our attitudes at work in our problems. "The environment, whether seen as powerful and unmanageable or as readily subject to control, may be regarded as supportive, hostile or dangerous." If we hold attitudes about our ability to master life tasks, these are beliefs that *limit our expectations.* If we hold an attitude of helplessness, we will expect to be at the mercy of possible dangers.

Figure 10-3

Levenson locus of control scale

Using the scale -3, -2, -1, +1, +2, +3, indicate the extent to which you agree or disagree with each of the following items, Let -3 represent complete disagreement and +3 complete agreement. Put the number representing the degree of your agreement or disagreement by each item. Directions for scoring your responses are given at the conclusion of the inventory.

1. Whether or not I get to be a leader depends mostly on my ability.
2. To a great extent my life is controlled by accidental happenings.
3. I feel like what happens in my life is mostly determined by powerful people.
4. Whether or not I get into a car accident depends on how good a driver I am.
5. When I make plans, I am almost certain to make them work.
6. Often there is no chance of protecting my personal interest from bad-luck happenings.
7. When I get what I want, it's usually because I'm lucky.
8. Although I might have good ability, I will not be given leadership responsibiity without appealing to those in positions of power.
9. How many friends I have depends on how nice a person I am.
10. I have often found that what is going to happen will happen.

11. My life is chiefly controlled by powerful others.
12. Whether or not I get into a car accident is mostly a matter of luck.
13. People like myself have very little chance of protecting our personal interests when they conflict with those of strong pressure groups.
14. It's not always wise for me to plan too far ahead because many things turn out to be a matter of good or bad fortune.
15. Getting what I want requires pleasing those people above me.
16. Whether or not I get to be a leader depends on whether I'm lucky enough to be in the right place at the righ time.
17. If important people were to decide they didn't like me, I probably wouldn't make many friends.
18. I can pretty much determine what will happen in my life.
19. I am usually able to protect my personal interests.
20. Whether or not I get into a car accident depends mostly on the other driver.
21. When I get what I want, it's usually because I worked hard for it.
22. In order to have my plans work, I make sure that they fit in with the desires of people who have power over me.
23. My life is determined by my own actions.
24. It's chiefly a matter of fate whether or not I have a few friends or many friends.

Scoring procedure for the I, P, and C scales

There are three separate scales used to measure one's locus of control: Internal Scale, Powerful Others Scale, and Chance Scale. There are eight items on each of the three scales. To score each scale add up your answers to the items appropriate for that scale. (These items are listed below). Add to this sum +24. (This removes the possibility of negative scores.) The possible range on each scale is from 0 to 48. Theoretically, a person could score high or low on all three dimensions.

Scale	Items	Interpretation
Internal scale	(1, 4, 5, 9, 18, 21, 23)	High score: indicates that an individual believes (s)he has control over his/her own life; Low score: indicates that an individual believes (s)he does not have much control over his/her own life.

| Powerful others scale | (3, 8, 11, 13, 15, 17, 20, 22) | *High Score: indicates that an individual believes powerful others have control over his/her life; Low score: indicates that an individual believes powerful others do not have much control over his/her life.* |
| Chance scale | (2, 6, 7, 10, 12 14, 16, 24) | *High score: indicates that an individual believes chance forces (luck) control his/her life; Low score: indicates that an individual believes chance forces do not control his/her life.* |

SOURCE: Levenson, H. 1974, "Activism and powerful others Distinctions within the concept of internal-external control," *Journal of Personality Assessment* 38, 381, 382. Reprinted with the permission of author and publisher.

Equally, "general beliefs about one's own power, or in the ultimate providence of the world, encourage hope under the worst specific conditions." Attitudes help a person cope in the most difficult of times, just as negative beliefs favor a pessimistic outlook even in the most favorable circumstances. Negative beliefs make it easier to have hopes dashed at the slightest provocation.

Suppose we look at three attitudes which in particular bear on you having staying power and coping with distress: 1) your attitude toward personal control; 2) your attitude toward dogmatism; and 3) your attitude toward tedium.

Attitude Toward Control. One of the most widely recognized attitudes today as being important for coping is that of personal control. One may believe that this control is within oneself, but one may also see that control as elsewhere. To see where you put personal control, pause for a moment and take the self-quiz in Figure 10-3

From this quiz you will recognize that people believe that the control of their own lives comes from any of three sources: within oneself, other people, or chance. If you scored high in inner control, you will cope with the energy and expectation that your efforts make a difference. If you scored high in other people's control, you will cope with the expectation of drawing on others or depending on them — using them as your main resource. If, finally, you scored high on chance control, you will cope with the expectation that nothing much you or anyone else does will make a difference; getting what you need or desire is pretty much a matter of chance.

A "dogmatic" attitude is similar to that of control in being one which registers our anxiety. It is an attitude which shows a lack of confidence, powerless, and a general belief that the environment is threatening. Researcher Milton Rokeach developed a scale of this belief which he calls *dogmatism*. He assumes that there is a way of coping with anxiety which is *closed-mindedness*. You may like to check yourself out on some of the items of this attitude, in Figure 10-4

Figure 10-4

Dogmatism

Man on his own is a helpless and miserable creature. T
Fundamentally, the world we live in is a pretty lonesome place. T
Most people just don't give a "damn" for others. T
I'd like it if I could find someone who would tell me how to solve my personal problems. T
At times I think that I am no good at all. T

An attitude which is reflected here reflects a person who is highly susceptible to anxiety. Such a person would hold the general belief that one's transactions with life events offer the continual promise of harm and danger. Such a person looks upon situations mainly as threatening, stressful.

Attitude toward tedium. We have fears from many possible directions. Consider the fears with which a person can wake and start his day. What would be these fears? Fear of another hassle with that fellow worker or set-to with one's supervisor? Fear of increasing distance between oneself and one's marriage partner. Fear the school will call again about one's child having problems. Fear of making as many sales, or more, than last week. Fear that one will not express self well enough. Or, fear that one will not have any new experiences on which to grow or thrive. Then of course there is that very simple fear, more present to some than to others: fear of one's own mistakes — will there be so many today?

But one special fear remains, the fear of *tedium*. This particular fear needs staying-power in a very special way. A key problem in any stress is:

    *How long can I put up with this stress

The problem in any stress is we become blinded — to seeing that the difficulty will ever end. No end is seen to be in sight. This fear of tedium is close to the Boredom we addressed earlier. It is today called "Burnout."

The fear of tedium is often expressed in this form (perhaps expressed early in the morning):

> Same ol' grind — day in and day out. How will I be able to face another day . . . and another . . . and another. It's not as if I'm facing some great problem, high risk or great loss. It's just the endless drag of _____ (e.g. my illnes, job, marriage, living quarters, etc.)

It is as if life has basically become a "lengthy" process. The biggest problem is that it is all stretched out as one very, very long drag. What is one's *attitude* toward the lengthiness?

THE IMPLICATION OF THE FIRST TWO TOOLS

Once you are aware of your needs and your attitudes in your distress which will not go away, you have made a major step in seeing what you can do about your situation. A first step, but it is not yet a solution. But knowing your needs and attitudes brings you to seeing that your solution will come from getting help from others.

It should be evident that changing some of your expectations may require the help of someone trained in these matters. Being aware of certain attitudes which are influencing your bearing up under your distress may suggest that these are attitudes which will be changed with the help of someone with special training. In brief, you may best bear up with your difficult dilemma, for so long as this is required, by the help of others.

In the most severe of dilemmas and distress you may need professional help, to help you work through your needs and attitudes. Self-help often is not sufficient for the most difficult of life's problems. The help of well-intentioned friend is frequently not the most adequate either.

Just a major point of such a self-help book as this is that we must depend on others (as in Chapter Two), so another point is that we must know the most helpful others to go to. Sometimes this is to go to professionals. This brings us to the third tool, your resources.

THIRD TOOL: KNOWING YOUR RESOURCES AND USING THEM

Some stresses are what we might call the Broke and Sued variety.

> Allen applied for a loan for bills.
> He owned nothing, had bills from a past marriage, and was attempting to go to school. He was turned down for the loan and at this most vulnerable of times, a man appeared at his door with a court judgment; he was being sued for not making payments on a car he had voluntarily given up a year earlier on the promise of the bank that they would have the car sold and thereby absolve Allen of any

debt. Allen had lost the letter to this effect in a fire. Now the bank wanted to force Allen out of school to pay the debt.

Allen depended on his lawyer to settle the court case and depended on a counselor to get his feelings out.

With a problem like Allen's, there are some stresses where the basic solution will not come from personal Short Order Solutions, like exercises of relaxation, but rather from *knowing where our resources are.*

In Allen's stress the resources are people, experts who are more knowledgeable in a field than he is and who can give him help he can get nowhere else. Stresses calling for resources include:

LACKS	RESOURCES
*Needs & Attitudes	*Mental Health professionals*
*Legal pressures	*Lawyers*
*Physical Handicaps	*Occupational Therapists*
*Unemployment	*Employment agencies*
*Hunger	*Food stamps*

There is nothing shameful about using these resources. Likewise there will be stresses where the resources include professional counselors: for personal feelings, for marriage difficulties, for continuing mood states. So we should not expect that the "self help" approach will work for all stresses. Part of being a good coper means knowing where our resources are, and using them. No less is this true of personal and emotional difficulties.

Today this tool has good news and bad news. The good news is that if stress is indeed more today, so also are people's resources. Even if our needs are harder to identify, as we have seen, most peole are also more able to be resourceful.

The optimistic fact for coping with future stresses is that mental resources are usually visible to most people. Most people are sophisticated due to mass media. They know about hotlines, phone numbers for help with crises, aid to dependent children, employment opportunities, battered wives, and the like. People are informed of resources. So we need not confuse sophistication with higher education or college degrees. Sophistication for coping with stress, thereby reducing vulnerability, is a question of being *informed*. And most people today are informed, or can be, of their rights, appeals, and social supports. That's the positive side of knowing about this vulnerability to stress. Mass media helps to make us less vulnerable.

At the same time, many people live in stress because they are not being resourceful. These stresses are particularly where people's basic survival needs and safety needs, indicated earlier, are threatened. People are in stresses because they are not using the resources available to them.

Unused Resources

In one of the country's largest cities, San Antonio, Texas, the stress of poverty is of greatest threat because people do not get what they need — they do not use their resources. One worker observes, "It's a characteristic of poor people not to seek assistance programs."

One in four of the county's 300,000 earns less than $10,000 a year in disposable income. Of these 80,000, low-income families, 15 percent receive welfare payments, but 85 percent do not; 50 percent receive food stamps, but 50 percent do not; 24 percent receive social security but 76 percent do not; 26 percent receive Medicaid but 76 percent do not.[1]

'Most of them don't want to get assistance, anyway," says one expert, because "they feel they can get by on their own."

Not using one's resources can be understood from a number of views: people do not want to depend on these, as we have just seen, and so part of their stress is lodged in a conflict between their need for their own initiative and getting their basic needs met. At other times, not using those resources is due to people not *knowing* where to seek assistance. At still others, the resources are wrapped up in red tape: the people know and are willing to use their resources but are frustrated because of bureaucratic barriers.

1. San Antonio Light, July 19, 1981 (p. 22 A)

Updating Resourcefulness

By and large, being more informed and mentally alert makes us less vulnerable to threatening stresses. Threats to safety as well as to other needs are lessened by vigilant, intelligent copers. Greater knowledge reduces ambiguity, minimizes feelings of being afraid.

At the same time, having perfect knowledge of our resources is usually a quest we have to seek. That is, knowing our resources perfectly is rarely fixed and perfectly achieved; we must try to continually update our knowledge of whom we can depend on — what people, what agencies or what skills in ourselves.

In this sense, keeping up on our resources is like keeping up with the fashions in clothes. Fashion is what comes in one year and goes out the other. It is what goes out of style as soon as most people have one. Resources are not fashions, but they do change and we must keep up with the changes. For example, United Way services produces a "Blue Book" of the different agencies caring for needs of the poor, the homeless, children, battered wives, and so forth. Because these agencies change (some closing down and others opening up), the Blue Book must be forever updated.

So it is with our knowledge of our own resources: the knowledge must be forever updated, or we must be in touch who are updated.

CONCLUSION

Let me conclude by mentioning a major issue for staying power in distresses which seem not to go away. Once you've assessed your needs and learned to change them, once you have highlighted your attitudes and used your resources, you will need to return to what your own staying power will force you to face, *sadness*.

STAYING POWER AND SADNESS

Staying power is the capacity to put ourselves in a state of "Hold." It is rather like the ability to idle your motor when you feel like stripping your gears.

I'm Doing My Best ... But It Isn't Enough

Staying power is an active power, an active ability and not passive inertia. Staying-power is needed for coping with stress because within every stress there is *sadness*. Sadness is really the big problem of life, a major ingredient in depression (as we have seen). Anything difficult causes sadness. The more difficult the problem, the greater is the sadness.

The result of being sad is to make a person want to abandon what he or she once wanted. The person without staying power reads into the signs of sadness an eviction notice. A sad person finds depression too high a price to pay, so packs up and leaves the neighborhood of what he or she once wanted.

Sadness makes a person stop wanting, desiring or even loving what he once did. Rather than love when it entails sadness, the person stops loving "cuts out" and runs away.

Sadness is probably the most devastating of all emotions. It is to a person's spirit what pain is to the body. A person in sadness is either in the process of giving up what she once valued or has already abandoned it. The sadness makes her lose her grip on what she once prized. If it goes on long enough, sadness will make a person less ready to fight and more prone to despair.

Staying-power is a capacity to withstand sadness. Staying power enables a person to continue to pursue a goal, maintain a loyalty even in the face of sadness.

Sadness means we are losing *hope*. Oscar Wilde once wrote,

> We were as men who in a den
>   Of filthy darkness grope:
> Something was dead in each of us,
>   And what was dead was hope.

Staying power is only possible so long as we have hope. Staying power then means we do everything in our power to see the chances of coming through our stress, at least as strong as we went into it. It is the power of those who are "survivors."

Sadness, then, also means a feeling of helplessness. A person seems without the strengths or resources which he or she once had. Staying power here means it is an Attitude of Reminding. One reminds oneself of moments of strength, instants of power or success. And most of all staying power is an attitude of reminding oneself that you are *not alone,* since loneliness is far and away the biggest cause of sadness. What you most need is hope. This hope comes from knowing and and using your resources, most of all resources of people.

TO OUR READERS: We welcome inquiries about our publications. In case your bookstore does not have that particular publication of ours that you desire, please order directly from us by mail, enclosing the list price plus $1.50 for mailing and handling.

Brunswick Publishing Company
Route 1, Box 1A1
Lawrenceville, Virginia 23868